IT'S A DAI

It's a Dad's Life

KEVIN MURPHY

MERLIN
PUBLISHING

Published in 2000 by
Merlin Publishing
16 Upper Pembroke Street
Dublin 2
Ireland

www.merlin-publishing.com

ISBN 1-903582-01-6

A CIP catalogue record for this book is available from
the British Library.

Typeset by Gough Typesetting Services, Dublin

Printed by Cox & Wyman Limited, Reading

This book is dedicated to my parents.

Contents

Introduction

This collection of my newspaper columns covers the first two years of my life as a househusband. Why did I give up my job to stay at home and mind our children? A good question. I have had many opportunities to ask myself this, and many times my untidy old desk at the newspaper has looked damned appealing!

People who work outside the home will tell you that their world is more or less an ordered place. People speak proper English to you. Requests are made of your time and attention that, on the whole, make sense. It is rare, although not totally unheard of, that colleagues turn into gibbering messes because they can't get their way. So, when things do happen in the outside world, they generally happen for a rational, logical, explainable reason. If they don't, you're usually talking about a good case for compensation.

By contrast, the way the home world works is like one long episode of "The Twilight Zone". I've included here a chapter of columns which sought to delve, explore, investigate and expose the very depths of this illogicality. Personally, I'd have settled for simply understanding it, but there you are.

When I gave up work in late 1996, the eldest was seven, Number Two was five and Number Three was three years of age. They have grown in that time which, I think you'll agree, is a remarkably astute observation on my part. But I have grown too. At first I grew fatter because I was eating everything in sight; then I got thinner because of the impossible strain it was putting, not on my marriage, but on the waistband of my trousers.

That's why I've given over a chapter to the subject of food. Being left alone in the house with a chocolate cake is a trial that not many workers outside the home ever have to face. But food also had its joys. My first tarts and my first breads coming out of the oven were Lennonesque moments.

And then, of course, there is school. When I worked in a newspaper office for a living I believed that the year was divided roughly into four seasons. From where I'm sitting now, I can see that this was a foolish delusion. The year is not divided into seasons: it is divided up according to school terms. When you have children the school year dominates, so I have devoted a chapter to this subject. During school terms there is an enormous amount of discipline and self-denial needed. You can't lie on in the mornings and in the afternoons you become a taxi-man ferrying them to and from their precious extra-curricular activities.

When you talk of school, the flip side of the year is holidays. That's why you'll find a separate chapter on this very effective form of househusband torture. If you think the school terms are busy, a househusband works even harder when holidays come around. We all know about Christmas, Easter and summer breaks, but then there are mid-term breaks which, in my opinion, are a particularly nasty and insidious practical joke played by the Department of Education. They know it's not funny and yet every year they persist in doing it.

One holiday period that requires its own chapter is Christmas. I love Christmas. I can always tell when the season of peace and goodwill is upon us because I generally start getting migraines. The excitement, the preparations, the build up, the nuking of puds in the pressure cooker, the carols at top volume on the Fisher Price machine, the Panadol – these are what make Christmas what it is. The things that don't make Christmas great are the TV ads that start in early November and bang away at you, day in day out. You'll see that I make a number of suggestions as to what should happen to people who put out their ads too early, but readers with a nervous disposition might want to skip those because they are a bit unsavoury.

Being at home with children is not just about particular times of the year, though. It's about the entire year and about all the extraordinary, everyday things that happen. There is a chapter on these and I suppose it is really about managing with kids. Here you'll read about things like trying to teach the youngest the basic principles involved in blowing her nose; getting a fist in the you-know-where from the same child; watching Number Two running around in front of guests with a false willy sticking out of her jeans; suffering grievous bodily harm while trying to share Number One's bed on a night when she couldn't get to sleep. It's all wholesome, family stuff, really.

And that's before we even come to the "entertainment" section. This is the official chapter where you're supposed to laugh. No, honestly.

Then, where would any self-respecting selection of writings about househusbanding be without a chapter on housework? If you stay at home to mind kids, housework is a reality. It's like those other great certainties in life: birth, death and taxes. It lies there waiting for you, all the time, and it has to be done.

In case anybody is left with the impression that being a househusband is all fun, I decided to save until last what could only be described as the dark side of all this staying-at-home stuff. And it's not pretty, either. When you are home full time, the children sometimes get sick and need minding. Sometimes they have to be taken to the doctor. And sometimes they destroy the doctor's surgery and your state of mind along with it. Also, when you're at home you're supposed to remember things, like your wedding anniversary. And when you talk about the dark side you also have to make mention of the "facts of life" too, don't you? I get edgy and sweaty and jumpy and nervous when the subject raises its head. I thought I'd be so cool and calm and collected when my turn came to answer the great sex education questions. As you will see, things turned out slightly differently.

So, is this what it's like being a househusband, I hear you ask? Yes, and much, much more. Welcome to my world.

Kevin Murphy

Chapter One

It's not so much "a funny old world" when you're a househusband, it's more like "The Twilight Zone"

The world can be a funny place when you're a househusband. Try this for size. I'm in the DART station with the children and I want to go three or four stops down the line. I ask the man behind the window for a return ticket for one adult and three children.

"Five thirty-five," says he.

Remember, I am Guardian of the Family Finances now, so it is my duty to question every price and to query every fare.

"Five thirty-five? That sounds an awful lot just for us," I say in my best let's-arm-wrestle-about-this voice.

He looks at me like I've just insulted his mother. He asks me again how many of us there are, so I tell him, for the second time.

He says grudgingly: "I'll give you a family day rambler ticket."

Filled with that pride which comes from having saved your family money, I told him that sounded just fine and asked how much I owed him?

"Five thirty-five," he said, without a hint of a smile.

At this moment the train entered the station, so like an eejit I paid over the money. As we pulled away, I could have sworn I saw him wave at me and smile.

The next day I took the three children for a swim. Number One made a huge deal about putting her swimsuit on under her clothes before we left the house. I told her it was a great idea and busied myself getting fifty-seven items of pool-related fun gear into two large ruck-sacks.

At the pool, Number One took off her clothes and, hey presto, she had no togs on! Was I pleased? Did my face look like an overripe tomato without the green frill on top? For penance, she had to swim in her mother's togs secured with a ponytail elastic to hold the straps tight.

A couple of days later my wife comes home and con-gratulates me for finally getting a hubcap for the car. A what? The hubcap, she says, that's been missing from the front wheel for four months!

I go outside slowly, holding on to things in case I fall down. There on the car is a brand new hubcap that I did not put there. I am not making this up. It is the cleanest part of the car and it is still there. I go out every day to look at it in case the aliens who brought it to me take it away again. I am planning to build a shrine around it and talk to JWT about the possibility of religious tours.

There have been other inexplicable encounters like this, but a pain has developed over my left eye so I need to go and lie down now. Otherwise I'd write about the miracle of the credit card or how my Number Two eats bread and jam with barbecue chicken. Let me just say this: when I worked all day in an office for a living, the world was a place in which things happened for reasons a person could understand.

*

I was tired, that's why I was grumpy. Who wouldn't be tired sitting in a car for an hour on a warm day? I hadn't driven anywhere, I'd just sat in it outside the front door testing a theory. The theory was this: delivery men only call when you're out. Since I was expecting a man to come and take measurements for a new piece of carpet in the hall, I reckoned there'd be a better chance he'd call if I was not physically in the house.

The children were very good about it. They ferried me out bits and pieces to keep me amused, all the time being careful not to be spotted by anyone in case the experiment was ruined. I opened a very testing Tupperware container, I put a half ponytail in Number Two's hair, I opened the silver lock on Number Three's Barbie box, I did Number One's Irish reading with her, and I caught up on some reading of my own.

As though knowing I was conducting an experiment, the carpet man never arrived. I have since had to make a second appointment. This was a great disappointment to me because I felt sure that I had conducted the experiment with the utmost care. Next time, I'll have to be more rigorously scientific in my approach and hire a video so the children stay indoors and out of sight the whole time.

Anyway, when I was back inside again, I was tired and, yes, I was grumpy. The three children were having a ball in the kitchen with a new game they'd invented. Number Three was sucking up water from a cup and spitting it at the other two. Much laughter and jollification, oh yes, until Frankendad's bulky shape darkened the doorway. I aimed my well honed grumpiness at Number Three, since she was holding the cup in her hands and had a fresh cheek-full of water ready to spit.

"Sucking and spitting water is wrong, please stop it and don't do it again!"

Number Two jumped to Number Three's defence. "Dad, she's only little, there's no need to be so grumpy!"

I replied with: "She has to know the difference between right and wrong!"

Number One jumped in then. "Dad she gets told all that stuff in her Montessori school!"

"Excuse me, I'm her father. I'm supposed to tell her the difference between right and wrong. It's my job! Not the Montessori school's!"

Just then the doorbell rang. I flew to answer it. Had my experiment worked? Was this the carpet man? Alas, my hopes were dashed; it was merely a weeping motor-bike courier who'd lost his way in suburbia. It happens. I dragged myself back into the sitting room and flopped down on the couch beside the others who were starting to watch *Peter Pan*.

"Anybody fancy going to the cake shop?" I asked, as a way of making up to them.

Before you could say Captain Hook Hates Crocodiles, the telly was off and the three of them had formed an orderly line at the front door, ready to go. We had a grand old time, we were the best of pals again and all was forgiven. And there, in the letterbox when we got back, was proof that I am a great scientist. The note said: "The carpet man called but you were out."

*

I was standing in the kitchen drumming on the biscuit tin listening to U2's "Discotheque" on the radio. It occurred to me that being a househusband must be pretty similar to being a housewife. Okay, you wouldn't wear the same clothes as a housewife, but you'll have similar kinds of daydreams, most of which have you escaping being a housewife, if you follow me.

I was daydreaming about playing on tour with U2 in the States. Up in lights I could see "U2's World Tour with Lots of Music and Famous Models and Cool People and Stuff" and underneath in smaller letters there was: "Special Guest: Kevin Murphy on Biscuit Tin". It might sound slightly odd to people who work outside the home full time, but I'm beginning to play a pretty mean biscuit tin.

But, as with most daydreams, it was shattered by reality. The doorbell rang. Granny and Granddad, who've been staying with us for a few weeks and about whom I am not permitted to write or else I'll lose my tongue and both my hands, shouted: "Doorbell!"

When I opened the door it was the carpet man, at long last. Call me fussy, but I'd always wanted a mat-well inside the front door because my lot make detours to find muck and dirt. This is the technical bit so, like the girl from "Friends" says in the shampoo ad, concentrate.

You lift the floor boards and put in a false bottom so that the scrubby mat sits level with the rest of the carpet. Okay? In my house, the hall is upstairs and the bedrooms are downstairs. I don't know why. It was like that when we got it. So when you lift floorboards in the hall there is just plasterboard underneath, which is the ceiling of the bathroom down below. With me?

I left these highly trained professionals to get on with the job and hid myself in a room to plan the day's menu for those-who-must-not-be-written-about. I was nearly asleep when I got my second reality check of the day. I've worked on enough building sites to know the sound of falling rubble very well. It begins with a large, loud crash and then is followed by short tinkly sounds and usually a groan or two – which is exactly what happened.

The carpet man had stepped into the mat-well before he'd put the mat-well in, if you know what I mean, and had crashed down through the ceiling of my bathroom. He didn't break any bones but he was severely shaken, not least his pride. His team of workers were very good about it, though, because not one of them laughed out loud.

As for me, I slid into a traumatic stress condition and curled up in a ball on the floor. After slapping my face a few times, to no effect, they just left me giggling and drooling in a corner with a blanket over me and got on with their work.

When I came around, Granny and Granddad were very sympathetic, which was kind of them, and then Granddad said he fancied some ice cream. I was about to hold him out of the top window by the ankles until he didn't feel like ice cream anymore, an idea I'd seen in *A Fish Called Wanda*, but the carpet man came in and said he and his lads were off. They all left promising to send a plasterer back to fix my ceiling; I don't know about you, but I believe the plasterer will come. Really, I do.

As for me and U2, well, the point of all this is that it wouldn't have happened if I'd been away on tour. Or maybe it would, but at least it wouldn't have happened to me because somebody else would have been here to cope with it, which is nearly the same thing as it not happening at all. I'm not saying being a rock star is easy but I just don't think it's as tough as what I'm doing. Which is why I've stepped up my practise on the biscuit tin. Don't laugh. I'm serious.

*

It's been a funny old week in many ways. I tried chocolate cheese for the first time ever. We now have bananas permanently hanging in our kitchen. The girls have formed a percussion band called Out Of This World which sends me Out of My Head. I had to rummage in the bins to prove that a two-headed pig was born. And the neighbour has a leak that no-one can fix. Just a regular week, really.

The chocolate cheese, as you might have guessed, was nothing short of disgusting. She-who-likes-a-good-laugh brought it home from a food exhibition. Germans made it. I dipped my finger in and it felt like yoghurt. I tasted it and it tasted like chocolate yoghurt, except I knew it was cheese and so I couldn't finish it. My advice to the Germans is: call it yoghurt and say nothing.

The bananas in the kitchen is a new fad which she-who-is-right-about-these-things has come upon. A bunch is hanging from a rail where I keep my utensils even as I write. The idea is that they'll last longer this way. We have tried putting them in various bowls but they've gone off as quickly as you can say "bananas in pyjamas are coming down the stairs", so the bright yellow fruits now occupy a prime position in my active little kitchen. Defying the intense heat and steam which my cooking tends to generate, they hang there probably reliving old memories of their hot and humid homeland, swapping tales from the plantation, sharing useful tips and information, the way bananas do. But, seriously, I think it might work. The bananas will last longer this way, but only because none of us will be able to remember where the flipping things are when we go to the fruit bowl looking for them.

As any parent will tell you, there's nothing like a banana to stuff up the mouths of children who want to sing songs and bash boxes all the time. Quiet is something in short supply in our house. The latest disturbance is this all girl band called Out of This World, subtitled "The Weirdest Band on the Planet". They are supposed to be alien rock stars, but don't ask me why. Apart from making up and singing the songs, they also have percussion instruments, just to be sure the noise is loud enough. There is a stone from Brittas Bay that is whacked vigorously with a big stick; there is a Frisbee Sellotaped to an empty shoe box; a wooden whistle; a red, plastic, squeaky clown's nose; and a tin spaghetti holder which has held its last spaghetti.

Every so often Out of This World is invited to get Out of My House when the jangling tones of its compositions threaten to unhinge my already fragile nerves. Since none of them have hall door keys and do not remember to leave the Yale lock on the latch, as soon as I've shooed them out they want to come back in again. I'm thinking of changing my name to Yo-Yo Murphy.

The strangeness of the week was carried through to a fascinating story in the paper about a two-headed pig born in South Africa, or somewhere outside Ireland. I happened to mention this to Number One some days later and she didn't believe me. I was highly offended by this and told her I'd prove it. After half an hour rummaging in the bins, much as a two-headed pig might do, I came up with nothing. So she still doesn't believe me. What's worse, Pierse next door thinks we've hit rock bottom and are reduced to eating scraps from the bin. I'm not going to go on about my overdraft any more because people take me too seriously.

Still with strange, the same Pierse has a leak in his roof than no-one can find. Some of the country's best-trained roofers have been up on his tiles and found nothing. More amazing even than that, it never leaks during heavy rain, only when it's that light, wispy, drizzly stuff. I suggested his house might be haunted by a baby and the leaks could be baby dribble but he didn't cheer up, for some reason.

As I like to tell the children now and again, when all the word seems weird and confusing, and there's no chocolate to hand, thank goodness for television. Or, to be more precise, "The Simpsons", "Sabrina – The Teenage Witch" and "Friends". They are fleeting oases of tranquillity in the constant chaos that is our life.

*

Now that I'm spending all day every day with my children I have come to learn that I need a strong stomach. I used to get the spins putting a Band-Aid on a scraped knee, but all that is changing. My innards are developing an iron coating from being around these children.

I'm not talking about things like Number Three's canny knack of needing her bum wiped when we're in the middle of a meal. I've learned to cope with that. No, the stuff I have in mind is a little more unsavoury.

The other day we drove to the shops. I parked in a car park and thought they were all following behind me. After a few steps I turned around to find them standing around something on the ground. When I went back to see what it was, it turned out to be a squashed rat.

"Isn't it cool," said Number Two.

I had my hand over my mouth trying to keep my lunch down and with the other I shooed them away from the offensive thing.

The squashed rat must still have been on their minds a couple of days later because, again in the car, a conversation started up about what it would be like to be run over by a steamroller.

Number Two wondered whether it would be worse to be run over from the feet or the head first. After much thought and reflection, Number One opted for head first because that way you'd be dead before the steamroller got to your feet. I could feel my stomach begin to lurch again, so I asked them to change the subject.

And then, no more than a week or so after Number Three's big toenail fell off, she went and did herself some more serious damage. The toenail, I should explain, has been going for about two months, ever since she dropped a torch on her bare foot. In the early stages, I thought I'd throw up when bathing and bandaging it. Little did I know there was worse to come.

Last week, having arrived home, I went to open the front door and heard a blood-curdling scream behind me. Parents of young children will know that there are two types of screams: there are the ordinary screams which you can take your time checking out, and there are the serious SCREAMS which make you drop everything and run – and this was such a case.

Number Three had slammed the car door on her thumb. Had it been anybody else's child I would have vomited first and then fainted, happy in the knowledge that there was someone else to cope with the situation. But there wasn't, so I had to do the soaking and bandaging and comforting, as well as keep my stomach under control. I aged five years that afternoon. And then, just when I'd stopped the flow of blood and was searching for bandages, two neighbours called around to ask if the trees at the back of the house bothered me at all. Funny old world, isn't it?

That night we had pasta for dinner and Number One thought I'd find it funny if she showed me how she could squeeze bits of pasta out from under her top lip with her fingers. My appetite just kind of left me after that.

Then we all got tummy bugs. The children were very good about this. They fell ill strictly in rotation, so that I had only one sick child to deal with at any time. When they all seemed to be clear of it, I was able to get out and do some shopping again, until Number Three threw up in one of the shops. Unfortunately, she saved most of it for the back seat of the car on the way home. The leftover smell of it in the car makes me feel nauseous. I hope it fades before the cold weather comes because driving around in winter with my head hanging out the window will not be any fun at all.

*

Good old Uncle Gaybo isn't aware of it but he gave our house the best laugh we've had in ages. The other week he had some of the eco-warriors from the Glen O' the Downs on "The Late Late Show", but myself and she-who-sometimes-shares-my-toothbrush were out and missed it. The following Sunday our neighbour Siobhain, who had seen the "Late Late", wanted to take our kids out with her kids for the afternoon. Wasn't that a great idea?

She telephoned and I could hear a plan being hatched with the mother of my children. The next thing the phone goes down and I can hear a rustling of the newspapers.

"That was Siobhain," the voice from the kitchen shouts to me.

"Oh, really," I said, "what's she up to?"

"She wants to take the children out."

"Excellent," I said, "I like Siobhain, I really do."

"She's taking them to see eco warriors."

"Even better," I said, "they'll enjoy that."

Then there was a pause and some more rustling of the newspapers.

"What cinema is that on in?"

Boy, did the other kids and I have fun with that. Woooeeee, we surely did! We laughed until our noses ran. Number One was laughing so hard she started making a snorty nose sound that worries me. I'd hate her to laugh like that at a work "do" when she's 25, but this time I let it go without comment. You know how touchy kids can be.

So there you are. *Echo Warriors*, a new movie starring Brad "I-live-a-tree" Pitt and Julia "I-need-a-bath" Roberts. And by the way it's not "Echo" warriors as in wrecko, it's "Eco" as in the "Meeko" of Disney's *Pocahontas*.

Speaking of trees reminds me of the first thing I did when I set out on the road to househusbanding. A big gale about a year ago knocked a huge branch off an old tree around the corner. Being a househusband without a full-time job anymore, nothing would do but to ask the good neighbour who owned the tree if I could have the huge hunk of fallen tree. For firewood.

I spent a whole afternoon lugging this stuff up the road in a battered old wheelbarrow. The kids danced around thinking this was a great lark. And the result? This half-tree lay in the front "yard", as a former childminder of ours used to call it, until very, very recently. She-who-knows-an-eejit-when-she-sees-one made me give it away, but I'm not going into that 'cos it's kind of humiliating.

But if you think that was bad, spare a thought for our pal John who works in a bank. John was walking in Stephen's Green on his lunch break and there were these men chopping up an entire tree which had fallen down.

Probably in the same wind. (Damn, I forgot to ask him that! That could have been the basis of a bonding experience!) Being a man with an eye for a bargain, John bought the entire tree and even got it delivered. And all for £40, or maybe it was £60.

Like me once, he now has a huge chopped-up tree in his garden. I can't tell you how impressed I was at this piece of male ingenuity. But there isn't one woman who agrees with me. My wife, his wife, and probably every other woman who's heard the story, thinks he's got something missing upstairs.

Undaunted, he's going to hire a chainsaw and chop the tree up into tiny pieces. When he mentioned this it brought to mind a story of another neighbour who was very lucky he was using his chainsaw while his partner was around. Very lucky.

So there you have it. My week, my life, my trees. The kids are fine, doing grand. One is on crutches for a sprained ankle, one cries every time she's asked to do something in the house, and one swears she didn't bite anybody in school and that she was framed. Life goes on.

*

People are always coming up to me and saying things like: "You're perfect – tell us the secret." No, really, it's true. They do. It's terribly embarrassing and it goes on nearly everywhere: in the supermarket, in church, in the bookmaker's. I always try and be humble about it but it's really hard. So I've decided to let out some of my trade secrets on how to be a perfect househusband in the hope that it'll stop people coming up to me on the street.

First of all, and this is the hard one, try and train yourself to dislike having lots of spare cash of your own to play with. I feel this is an essential requirement for any man who wants to take househusbanding seriously. Too much money is only a distraction. It makes you itchy to go out shopping and spend, spend, spend. This, in turn, means you take your eye off the important core issues, namely the children, the house and the "Oprah Winfrey" show.

The second most important thing is to try and loosen up a little about your personal appearance. Going through life without a hair out of place, if you're unfortunate enough to be hairy, is too much of a strain when you have kids to mind. The day you look in the mirror and pride yourself on your neat appearance is the day you get a jammy handprint on your cool black Wranglers. Remember, neatness is the path of vanity and folly, so always choose the other route. Be prepared to deliver the children to school and chat to all the parents and teachers with toast on your chin or drool on your shoulder. It is the way of things. They will understand.

The third golden rule, ripped at random from my best-selling "Ye Olde Househusband's 101 Infallible Tips", is to always, *always* bring a mini alarm clock around with you. Falling asleep in the middle of the day is only a bad thing if you sleep too long. I have found, from almost four per cent of a lifetime's experience, that between ten and twenty minutes is the ideal amount of time. Anything over twenty minutes and you risk grogginess, grumpiness and disorientation for the rest of the day. Don't be tempted, as I was when I started out, to fill in gaps in the children's schedule by doing useful things. No, resist this. If One is at piano, snooze in the car while you wait. If Two has a friend over, snooze on the couch while they play. If Three is at a party, go to bed. Not only will it restore the much-needed sleep you lose most nights, but it is also good for the complexion.

Obviously, I can't list every iota of knowledge I have gleaned from my long year-and-a-bit as a househusband, but I hope that some of you will have learned something very valuable today from these "choice cuts" of wisdom, as my local butcher might say. Remember, as the primary housekeeper and homemaker, you make the beds every day and so you're entitled to lie in them.

Speaking of local shops, I went to get the trousers of my only suit taken out and the lady never even bothered to measure me. She just looked me up and down and said she'd let out as far as it was humanly possible to let out a pair of trousers. I'd had to buy a Snickers bar on the way home to console myself. Well, recently I had another repair job carried out on the same trousers by the same lady. When I got them home, what do you think was in the pocket? Absolutely right: a Snickers bar. Is that the cruellest thing you ever heard? And this was in the middle of Lent. Like a river in a desert, the chocolate is such an unusual sight that we have given it its own cupboard in the kitchen. At regular intervals we take turns to visit it and just look. An uneaten Snickers is a rare thing in our house and for that reason it is quite a curiosity. Even she-who-claims-that-I-snore-with-drink-taken has been found standing at the cupboard sighing to herself. Short of snaffling it for myself and then sneaking out to buy a new one to replace it, I can't see how I'm going to have that Snickers this side of April. Wait! What am I saying? That's a brilliant idea!

*

My car radio is on the blink, but Number Three had a great solution this week. She said I should get a TV in the car. She says it's boring driving around every day. I agree, but if we had a TV in the car, it wouldn't be fair on me, would it? I'm the one who has to do the driving and I'm the very one who wouldn't be able to watch the TV because, if I did, we'd crash.

Oh, yes, I've heard the argument that I could always watch it while waiting for one or other of them at swim-

ming, ballet, gym, piano, French, soccer, Swahili, or whatever. Very clever, except that it would interfere with my
naps. What use would I be to anyone if I didn't have my
naps?

So, we're not going to get a TV in the car. Anyway,
we need to get away from the box, not watch more of it.
The car is the last TV-free sanctuary known to man. It's
a bit like a wildlife preserve, I suppose, except it's on
wheels and costs a fortune to run. Sitting into a car is to
experience how life used to be before TV came and busied up our lives (and brought you-know-what to our holy
land). Keep cars TV-free, that's what I say. As a family,
it's the only place we get to talk anymore. Number Three
is not happy with this. She thinks it's about money and
there's no convincing her otherwise.

The second predictably odd request this week came
from Number One. Instead of the name which she was
given at birth and the one of which both her mother and
I are very fond, she announced that she wanted to be
called "Adidas". Now, while Adidas Murphy does have a
kind of ring to it, it is not a name I want to be heard
shouting out loud in the supermarket or at night when
it's time for them to come in. As soon as she said it, I
could see myself standing at the front door yelling:
"Adidas! Come in! Your dinner's poured out." No, thank
you.

When I enquired why she had chosen Adidas, Number
One told me that a girl in third class was called "Reebok".
In her eight-year-old mind, this was the height of cool. I
told her that I would call her Adidas if she really, really
wanted, mainly because it is not an uncommon thing in
our house. Numbers Two and Three regularly ask to be
called different names at different times. Sarah and
Gloriana are two which spring to mind. But I have told
Number One that if this fashion catches on and the other
two start asking to be called Puma and Nike, I will have
to draw the line.

Speaking of changing things, Dana International's win in the Eurovision song contest sparked an intense discussion in our house about transsexuality. Number One and her cousin Hannah had no end of information about what the operation involves and how hormones are used to stop a man's hair growing and make his voice higher. As for the addition of the boobies and the subtraction of the willy, they had very firm notions of how this was done and didn't bat an eyelid when telling me about it. Interestingly, when Number One watched Eurovision she picked out the Dana International song as the best, long before the voting started. But, hey, that's just me bragging again.

Still on the subject of change, or the potential for change, the same two children asked me the other day who the man was who didn't want peace.

"Which man is that?" I asked.

"The man in the North who doesn't want there to be peace," they said.

"I don't think there's any man like that," I replied.

"There is, we saw him on the TV, he's big and shouts a lot," Number One said.

"Oh, you mean Ian Paisley," I offered.

"That's him, yeah. Why doesn't he want peace?" the cousin asked.

Where do you begin to explain the likes of Ian Paisley to children?

"I just think he's one of those people who doesn't like a lot of things," was the best I could do.

There was a pause as they mulled over this. Then the cousin said: "He's a funny guy."

"Yeah," said Number One, "he's weird."

*

I suppose "Blue Peter" thinks it's very funny. If it really is "Blue Peter" that's responsible. The eldest received a chain letter the other day. I was about to throw it in the bin when she pointed out that it claimed to be from "Blue Peter", the BBC children's show. They want to make the "Guinness Book of Records" for the longest chain letter. They should try the record for parents' curses.

The child jumped at the chance to help out "Blue Peter", so much so that she lay awake worrying in case she didn't send off her letters within the four-day deadline. She had to send six letters to six of her friends. Obviously, the original letter had to be photocopied six times and signed by her, but she also had to put five addresses of previous senders on the back of each envelope. Oh, and then we had to send a postcard to the first name on the back of the envelope she received. I kid you not, this took up an entire morning, half of it spent trying to understand the damned instructions. To put it mildly, it left us all a little stressaroonied.

After we'd bought the stamps and checked the phone book for the right addresses and posted the blasted things, she asked: "Can I tear up my chain letter now?"

"You certainly can," I said.

"I'm going to enjoy this," she said, ripping it up into the bin.

I can safely tell "Blue Peter" or anybody else thinking of getting us to do another chain letter that they have two chances in this house. I also had to explain my initial reaction to the child. I had wanted to bin it because chain letters are used sometimes to con people out of money.

"How do they do that?"

"They get you to send them money instead of a postcard."

"Hey, that's a great idea," she said, her eyes lighting up again.

"I know," I said, "we'll try it when you're older and your handwriting's better."

Now, from "Blue Peter" to blue shorts. I have decided

that I am going to wear them until the end of August. Not the same pair continuously, mind you. They will be washed at regular intervals and I will have other pairs to wear while that is happening. And I will take them off at night when I go to bed, honest. No, the point is that I am going to defy this lousy weather that we call the Irish summer. I am going to shake my fist at the cloudy, grey skies and stride about the place in shorts, with bare legs. It is all I can do to stop myself sliding into the rain-laden slough of despair. People will laugh at me. They might even throw rotten fruit at me. But the steel vice that is my disciplined mind has closed shut on this issue. I will not be moved. Besides, I might get away with half fare on the buses.

The other day we went to Marley Park in Rathfarnham and the instant we got to the playground, which is a two-day hike from the main entrance, the rain began. I took all the raincoats out of the rucksack that is surgically attached to my shoulders and, once I'd got them all on the girls and zipped up, the sun came out. So then the kids were too hot and we had to take the coats off again; once I'd had them all off and packed away into the rucksack, it began to rain. I started to wish I was on our disastrous holiday in Spain again. In fact, it was worse than that. I started to wish I was Spanish.

Let me make a few suggestions here to people who have lots of money and are looking for something that will make them even more money: build a water park, with enormous slides, pools and wave machines in the Dublin area. Kerry has one. So does Kilkee in County Clare. It's indoors, so it's weatherproof and it would be something my kids would want to do every day of the week. Useful hint: keep it spotlessly clean, run it efficiently and don't charge an arm and a leg.

My second free business tip is this: an indoor play arena with air conditioning, so parents can breathe and the children don't dehydrate. Even a window that opens would be nice. Useful hint: keep it spotlessly clean, run it efficiently and don't charge an arm and a leg.

Or, to be even less specific, suggestion three: anything with a roof over it.

*

Maybe it's part of the culture, but I hate being penalised. The reason I mention this is that my other half, the one you'd have to be up pretty early to put one over on, has instigated a new penalty system in the house to ensure compliance with the rules. I think she's been reading too much about this car-clamping business. Anyway, now that I'm eating nothing but healthy stuff, and now that I'm bright eyed and bushy tailed because of a temporary diet-induced drink-free existence, she's getting irked by some of my new lifestyle habits. Absolute top of the list is the leaving of apple cores lying around.

I agree, it can be pretty yucky to put your hand on a cold, squishy, just browning apple core, but I can remember a time when I used to smoke and we'd have been talking about cigarette butts, not apple butts. But does that make any difference? Not a whit.

I am now to be fined £5 every time I leave an apple core in the car. The slightly autumnal whiff of decaying apple flesh is not something that fills her mind with sentimental images of childhood. It's my own fault. I chose to marry a city dweller. I went into it with my eyes open.

I was in a cold sweat the other night over the new system. I'd just locked the front door and was about to turn out the lights when I remembered I'd left a core in the door pocket of the car. If she didn't exactly find it, she was going to smell it out first thing in the morning.

The problem was, how was I going to get out of the house at that hour of the night to retrieve the offending detritus without her twigging to what I was doing? The car keys make an awfully loud jingling noise and it's a sound that she can hear no matter how far away she is.

Technically, at that moment in time, I was in breach of the new rule. I had forgotten about the core and had left it in the car, even though I had remembered it and was trying to get it back, if you follow me. Mitigating circumstances count for nothing in our house. Just because I'd washed the kitchen floor earlier and we were now able to see its original pattern after all this time wasn't going to cut any ice. In the end, my salvation came in the unlikely form of a chicken carcass.

God works in mysterious ways. I'd made chicken stock earlier that evening from the remains of a roast chicken and the carcass had been dumped unceremoniously in the kitchen bin. This was enough to justify my going outside to the bins. And the noise of the plastic Crazy Prices rubbish bag drowned out the jingling of the car keys. It was a close shave and I don't want to go through it again.

Like apple cores, another of my habits now nearing its sell-by date is putting on my seat belt while driving down the road. Personally, I like this habit. It has all the macho elements that I look for in a good old personalised, exclusive to me, trait. It just seems to send out a message which says: "Look, I can do two things at once" or "I lead such a busy life that I haven't time to put the belt on before I drive off". But I will not be allowed to enjoy this Bohemian quirk anymore. I now have to pay the same amount of money if, and I'm quoting from the Murphy House Book of Rules and Regulations, "all four wheels of the family vehicle have left the drive and are in contact with the road in front of our house and no seat belt is on the bald guy we know as Dad".

And in case you think it is just me who's been getting it, think again. Number Two is now fined 10p every time she's caught sucking her thumb. After only the first week of the new regime, she's down 20p and she doesn't like it one bit.

So far Numbers One and Three have escaped, but they can't afford to get cocky. Number Three's endearing habit of pinching her sisters' arms is an ideal candidate for this system. So is her formerly cutesy way of asking for things followed by an abrupt "now". And Number One's habit of going temporarily deaf when asked to help with a job that does not involve singing, dancing, wearing new clothes, watching TV or eating sweets is just asking for it.

*

Do I look like I embarrass easily? I gave up my job to do girly work, but did I worry about what people would say? I gave up a business that's more macho than a bullfighter's undies and swapped it for one where you wipe noses a lot. Did I get embarrassed about it? The answers to these questions, respectively, are "no", "no" and "no".

But I got seriously embarrassed this week. Oh, yes. I got the big kahuna, the reddener of reddeners, the scaldy of scaldies, the morto of mortos. I'd taken Number Three down to collect Numbers One and Two from school. We arrived early and we were goofing about in the playground. Number Three found a little branch of a tree with lots of leaves on it and started to give it to me for a present.

"Here's a present for you, Dad," she said.

"Oh, thank you, that's lovely."

"No, actually, I think I'll give it to Mum."

"Awww," I groaned in a sing-songy voice.

"Okay, you can have it."

"No, I don't want it now."

"Go on, I was only kidding. You have it."

"No, you've hurt my feelings."

We were enjoying this game and when I turned my back she stuck the branch into my back pocket. I left it there and walked off to the school door to wait for the other two while she played in the yard. I got talking to some of the mothers and we were nattering about this and that. After a while another mother joined us. And she said those words that every man in female company dreads to hear.

"God, Kevin, you've a big bush hanging out of your trousers."

How can I describe my reaction? Okay, that's easy: I nearly died. I thought she meant, you know, that I was undone, hanging out, peeping through, leaning at an open door, enjoying the sunshine on the doorstep. You know what I mean. I was in a group of young mothers and I felt like, well, Bill Clinton, to be honest about it. My heart skipped a beat, I broke out into a sweat and my hands were making their way down to the free kick position for a quick security check when suddenly I remembered the damn branch in my back pocket.

But – ha, ha – it was too late then. Too late to – ha, ha – laugh it off. My face told the story. They knew I'd got the wrong end of the stick, or the branch in this case. It's not often I'm without a few words of repartee to fire back, but in this particular instance I was flummoxed, struck dumb and totally blitzed.

I still have that branch. It's stuck on top of a picture on the wall at home. It is a reminder of my biggest embarrassment as a househusband. It is also a reminder to check all the doors and windows before I leave the house in future.

Valentine's Day came and went in a flurry of love hearts and cards and flowers and kisses and hugs. She-who-likes-pancakes got one or two things too. But Number One got a personalised card all for herself. I am still reeling. She's nine. It arrived the night before, delivered by hand, at eleven o'clock. I tried to be cool, play it down and not make a big deal about it, but I suppose she got an inkling of my feelings when I shredded the teacloth with my teeth as she opened it. Not that I'm against boyfriends or valentines or anything like that. It's just that I hadn't reckoned on them arriving on the scene so early. When she's got a job and drives her own car is time enough, isn't it? I'm going to have to meet the young man's parents and find out what his intentions are. I'll also need to know if they have any money because, let's face it, this is important. And, thirdly, I'll need to know what he wants to be when he grows up. Soldier, sailor, fireman and Garda are out. Brain surgeon, pop star, Hollywood actor and Premier League footballer are in. Not that I'm pushy, you understand, but somebody has to look out for the kid's interests. All this lovey-dovey stuff is fine but you need some cash in the equation too.

*

It's happening already. Fame is beginning to rear its ugly head. Pretty soon I'll be getting invited out to places to autograph tea towels and oven gloves. After that it'll be a dizzying round of TV talk shows, top hotels, champagne breakfasts and offers of free washing powder. If I play my cards right, I'll get rich enough to hire an army of minders so I won't even have to see the kids. Yeeesss!

Okay, alright, maybe I'm getting carried away a little. We were at a party the other night and she-who-can-manage-quite-well-without-my-company was chatting away to friends when some people beside her started wondering out loud if the baldy guy on the other side of the room was You-Know-Who.

She turned to see who was doing the asking and naturally got sucked into the conversation. Was he the guy who writes for the "Sunday World", you know, the eejit who stays at home minding the kids and then writes about it, slagging off his poor wife? Poor wife? I had to laugh at that! Don't they know how much a bath of goat's milk costs? So, she-who-has-impeccable-taste-in-men said, yes, he was one and the same person.

"Do you know him?"

"Oh, I know him alright," she said, stifling a yawn. "I'm she-who-must-be-encouraged-to-continue-working."

I'm only sorry I wasn't there for that moment. Some things in life you just want to experience directly and not have told to you second hand. That chance will probably never, ever come round again. I want to be up close to people when they are gobsmacked, you know? Fame's not much good unless you're there to enjoy it. Now I know how Elvis feels. Felt. Or would have felt... Oh, never mind. I'm upset now.

But not half as upset as the Irish rugby team after the England game, mind you. I feel I owe the nation an apology. I'm afraid my children and their mad cousins were partly responsible for the poor performance of the team. I wasn't going to mention it but the guilt just won't go away. You see, the week of the game the whole Irish team was holed up in the Glenview Hotel at the Glen O' The Downs in County Wicklow. It just so happens that we were there, too, for a mega, extended family, relations-coming-out-of-your-ears gathering. We noticed at dinner that the water in the glasses kind of vibrated, but we thought it might be thunder. Little did we know it was Paddy Johns, Peter Clohessy and Keith Wood coming down the stairs. Naturally, the kids spotted them first and of course this set off a mass autograph hunt. My two older ones have the entire team's autographs on two scraps of cherished paper. And they got posters and stickers from the players, too.

But the point I'm getting to is this. The exertion of being chased around that hotel by a gang of seven autograph-hunting kids obviously took too much out of them. I watched the game on TV and every time they fumbled a pass or missed a tackle, I felt guilty about it. Their wrists were obviously weakened from writing out their names so many times. But nobody else would have understood what was happening except me. I had half a mind to ring the Irish Rugby Football Union before the game and get them to postpone the match – but who would have believed me? As it was, I decided to let the thing go ahead. I mean, the tickets were sold and everything.

As well as being lashed by England, we also mourned the passing of the milk bottle at our house this week. If it hasn't already happened in yours, then it will. No more the cheery shape of those glass soldiers with their red caps standing to attention on my doorstep in the mornings. Instead, anonymous cartons with the personality of a burst balloon.

But don't think we don't know what's going on here. Premier Dairies might think they're oh-so-clever, but in the Murphy house we know what their little game is. These cartons are so damned awkward to open that the children spill half the milk in the process. When that happens, who has most to gain? Exactly: the milk company. Do you get the gist of what I'm talking about here? A conspiracy on a huge scale, a national scandal, that's what. There's going to be such an increased demand for milk that the poor cows will be worn out. I wouldn't mind so much if the cartons had more of a personality about them. You could have a relationship with glass milk bottles. The cartons just aren't interested.

*

My legal team is being assembled at this very minute. The Hardimans, the McEntees, the Shipseys, they're all queuing up to get involved, their hot little faces twitching with excitement at being part of the mother of all constitutional challenges.

Why? Because my world has been rocked. Bun-rocked, in fact.

Yes, in idle moments, I have been reading our Constitution. In the gaps between wiping bums, Hoovering
the smoke alarm and doing the shopping, I have been
trying to better myself. Trying to lift myself from the
drudgery of existence with a little book learning.

But what do I find? I find that in the eyes of the State
I am a non-person. I have no right to be doing what I
am doing. I am the wrong sex. I am Nowhere Man.

Go to Article 41 and see for yourself. It's the one that
says the family is the indispensable basis for the welfare
of our entire society.

Check out paragraph 2.1º – it's just before the divorce amendment that allows the indispensable basis
for the welfare of our society to be broken up. Women
will know it, but here it is for male readers out there. It
says: "In particular, the State recognises that by her life
within the home, woman gives to the State a support
without which the common good cannot be achieved."

Was I angry when I read this? I nearly ripped up my
Marigold rubber gloves! *Woman* gives the State a support? Have you seen the condition of my hands? Don't
they realise I now walk with a permanent stoop from
picking up toys?

The consequences for all househusbands are horren-
dous. This means that because I am not a woman, and
have no intention of becoming one in the future, I am on
terrifically thin ice.

If my previous employer gets it into his head to haul
me back to the workplace, all he has to do is take a High
Court action and I'm done for. Imagine. Back to that life
of expensive restaurants, international travel, rubbing
shoulders with the rich and famous ... which wasn't so
bad, now that I think about...

But no, I will not weaken! I am Housespouse, Base
Guy, Domestic Engineer, Him Indoors, and proud of it!

That's not to say this little matter is going to go away
if we ignore it. Gather 'round brothers, the lawyers don't

come cheap and this is an hour of need. The Constitution needs a-changing and that will take money. Send as much as you can, as quick as you can, in unmarked notes to me at Boozy Bank, Ben Dunne Plaza, Cayman Islands. Don't be put off by the address, it's just a tax efficient thingy which my accountants insist on.

Don't be afraid of the challenge, either. I feel we can win this one because right is on our side. We homeboys have a right to be recognised under the Constitution. When you think of the amount of work we do, it's the least we can expect.

*

My middle child put a strange request to me this week. Would I put dog pooh in the paper? I'd never considered it before and my first reaction was that it might be a messy operation. Until I realised she wanted me to write about it rather than actually do it.

She was out walking with her friend and her friend's Mum and between them they counted 120 doggie doos on the path between our house and the local park. As soon as I heard this I just knew it was an absolute record because my own personal best is just 78. Naturally, I fired off a letter to the "Guinness Book of Records", but so far I have not had a reply. How these people can be so slow when exciting new records like this are presented to them I will never know.

I don't say this because I hate being beaten, but the child's total must have included the path outside the park because, using my advanced dog-turd-o-meter, it seems an unusually large number to me.

Our park is a lovely place where happy dog owners let their mutts run riot. Often they are both having such fun that there is very little to distinguish between human and dog, what with their wet noses and tongues hanging out. Except the humans know how to whistle and the dogs don't.

The fun part is always when we come back from the park. The excitement as we all leave our shoes and the buggy outside the house, so that I can wash the you-know-what off, has to be seen to be believed. Truly, it's the part I look forward to. I have a special suit that I got at a Sellafield discount sale last year. It comes with a screw-on helmet and extra thick gloves made of a kind of flexible metal. The neighbours think I'm a fussy neurotic. Just because I use a high-powered hose that pumps pure disinfectant?

What they don't realise is that I enjoy it. Let's face it, isn't it all part of what being a modern parent is about?

Call me weird, but I just happen to believe dogs should be allowed to do it wherever they want. And I also think dog owners should be allowed to look the other way while the mutts are doing it. I mean, if we start putting restraints on where dogs can pooh, where will it end? Strip-searches when you go to buy a six-pack? A passport check when you cross from one side of the Liffey to the other?

And have you seen those pooper scoopers? They are so uncool and unfashionably ugly! What self-respecting citizen would carry one of those things around when walking the dog, I ask you?

Yes, I know I'm being radical, but think about it. We have the possibility of an immense tourist attraction here, right under our noses, if you'll pardon the pun.

We could ship in the Continentals who are forced by crazy laws to carry those ungainly scoopers with them all the time. We could market special holidays and aim them at high-spending German or French doggie owners. Change the colour of the new tourism logo from green to brown, add a few more Mr Whippy curves, and you're halfway there already. Call the holidays "Scooper-Free Fortnights in the Emerald Isle" or something. They'd jump at the chance to walk their dogs and have one hand free, no question about it.

You could also have special guided tours around favourite doggy doo sites, where we could run quizzes with titles like "Guess That Dog". Or we could find out if the dogs belong to famous people, even half-famous people, and rename the park "Toilet to the Dogs of the Stars" or something equally catchy.

I don't know, opportunities are being wasted here which means some non-canine somewhere is not doing his little jobby properly.

Chapter Two

I always suspected there wasn't enough food in the world for me to eat but now I believe it

The Hoovering was done, the dusting was complete, the children's homework was finished and all the shiny surfaces had been thoroughly Jiffed. That was the problem.

There I was, at a moment when I should have been in my black Marigolds scrubbing my way round the house, miles ahead of my schedule and with nothing to do. A whole half an hour stretched in front of me before I needed to start cooking the dinner.

It's not a happy situation to find yourself in, especially when you're new to the homemaking game like I am. Feelings of worthlessness and deeply rooted insecurity begin to creep over you. It's not a pretty sight and to cap it all I couldn't find the Atrixo.

Then it dawned on me. The real reason I was getting so shaky was because I was sitting in the kitchen twiddling my thumbs while the remains of a chocolate cake, baked by she-who-must-be-encouraged-to-continue-working, sat eyeing me from the worktop.

At first I felt nothing but hostility for it. I hated its luscious icing and its moist brownness. But then I weakened and began to feel sorry for it. I imagined it lay like a wounded soldier on a battlefield, begging me to put it out of its misery before dinner time, after dinner being insufficient for some reason best known to itself. But isn't that always the way with chocolate cakes?

So, because I hate to see anything in pain, be it human, animal or chocolate, I quickened its end. And that, as I thought, should have been the end of it.

To my horror, I find that this one simple act of human kindness has now flung me onto the horns of a very painful dilemma. Do I follow up on my plan to learn to bake? Or do I leave that to my working wife?

Already I have found myself thumbing through Delia Smith's cookery book on how to make shortcrust pastry. In unguarded moments, my fingers have begun practising that "mingling in" marg and flour motion without me noticing.

But if I learn to bake, what will be the consequences? A house full of cakes and buns, and a wardrobe with no clothes that fit me? If I weaken in the presence of a half-eaten chocolate cake, then quite obviously I have a particular discipline problem here.

I'm not going to be panicked into any quick decisions. There's only one way to get over this and that's practise, practise, practise. I'm going to draw up a strict schedule and force myself to stick to it. One chocolate cake per week will be a tough regime but I'm going to beat this. If I don't, it won't be for lack of trying.

*

I made my first tarts this week. Two steaming apple jobs came out of the oven perfectly. It must have been like this for John Lennon when he baked his first bread during his househusband phase. Me, I've baked brown bread before but I'd never baked a tart. Get serious, this was something I could eat.

Admittedly I had help from she-whose-baking-talents-are-not-mortal but most of it I did myself. I fumbled a bit at the start trying to get the apron on but things settled down after that.

And then, after twenty minutes at 220ºC, the tarts were taken out of the oven, all browned and steamy and aromatic, looking like a massive childhood flashback, and placed on the sitting room table to cool. All and sundry were then invited to witness the masterly effort which I, a mere man, had made.

Neighbours who happened to be passing were collared and led in to see the miracle with their own eyes so that they could tell of it to their children and their children's children. Door to door salesmen, who seemed to want to leave very quickly for some reason, were given a viewing. A furniture delivery man who called to the wrong house was also brought in, as were two Seventh Day Adventists, one Hare Krishna who'd lost his mates, and the neighbour's dog, Timmy, who was allowed sniff but not lick.

In short, if my week could be summed up in one word, then that word would have to be "achievement". I had reached the househusband's Holy Grail. Not only that, but I'd served it up to my family with fresh whipped cream after dinner. The children's moony eyes and groans of delight were reward enough for all the hard work. Before you could say "I need a sleep on the couch now", the tarts were gone, the plates were clean and their just-baked perfection was but a dim and distant memory. But I won't forget. No, I'll never forget my first tarts, nor the first moment I saw them emerge, perfectly formed, into the world.

As with all silver linings, there is always a cloud. My barber, I discovered this week, is big into golf. In fact, it would be no small exaggeration to say that if a gun was put to his head and he was made to choose between home, family, with his barber's business thrown in, and golf, he'd pick golf.

In the mirror I could see my three asleep behind me on the leatherette armchairs. The medical profession should try experimenting with golf conversations when carrying out mega surgery. My theory is that it's nature's finest anaesthetic, numbing the brain, the spinal chord and all major nerves in the body. All you need is the surgeon to stand over you and tell you about his last game.

The word "barber" reminds me of a shameful episode during the week which could have overshadowed my achievement on the tarts front were it not for my ability to completely blot out unsavouriness whenever it occurs. We were driving along and Number Three was annoying the other two. She wouldn't let them sing their song, even though it was their turn. After many polite requests for her to stop, I snapped. I reached back and grabbed her mermaid Barbie, rolled down my window and held the doll outside the speeding car.

"If you don't let them sing the song, Barbie goes out the window," I said.

Have you ever heard of such cruelty before? I shocked myself. Even Barbie's steely grin turned to a grimace for those hair-raising seconds – and, boy, does mermaid Barbie have hair. It made Number Three do what she was told but I certainly didn't feel good after it. I hope Childline aren't reading this or I'm in big trouble.

*

Me and my big mouth. I happened to mention earlier, just casually, that I'd baked apple tarts, and suddenly the world and his wife knows about it. Can nobody out there keep a secret? This has put serious pressure on me because there's a cake sale coming up at the school and everybody's looking at old blabbermouth here to bake something really special. I just don't think I can take the pressure anymore.

This school has had more cake sales than any other in the civilised world. How would they like it if the local bakery started teaching children to read and write? Not a lot, I suspect. It's trying to raise £75,000 to build itself a new school building. By my calculations, that's about 37,000 cakes at roughly £2 each, which is a lot of dough either way you look at it. Up to know I've been able to get away with making little squares of fudge packed in plastic bags labelled: "Ye Olde Househusband's Fudge." Pretty neat, huh?

But not anymore. Now I've gone and put my rump end in the sling which has catapulted me into the big time. We're talking Boiled Fruit Cake minimum, here. That's what's keeping me awake at night. I keep seeing boiled fruit cakes flying around the bedroom, dive-bombing me, as I lie in a frenzied sweat wondering: should I do it, will I do it, can I get out of it?

The day of reckoning is coming. It's payback time for all my bragging. Only the Man Above knows whether I'll have what it takes to make it through. But know this, people, when I don my baking gear and step up to that mixing bowl, it's more than just a cake I'll be baking. This is about pushing out the boundaries of househusbanding, stepping into the unknown with nothing but a wooden spoon for protection, and going where no man in his right mind has ever gone before.

Forget your night classes in "How to be a Better Parent". The next time Dublin Zoo is holding courses for zookeepers, I'm signing on. I've suddenly realised the downside of being a stay-at-home parent. You go soft on the kids. I'm not joking. The noise level in our house now compared to when I gave up career and full-time employment is like comparing the noise level in the local library with a Spice Girls concert.

These kids don't talk any more: they shout. They can't explain something any longer: they have to put it to you in a song. They can't walk: they have to run. They can't sit still long enough to eat their meals: they have one foot on the ground ready to run back out to play. I don't know what to do. It's like living with a house full of hearing-impaired Olympic sprinters on steroids who shout all the time.

The other morning at breakfast they all came into

the kitchen and the first thing that happened, apart from the noise level rising, was Numbers One and Two wanting to sit in the same seat. There was much shoving and pushing and complaining over this seat. By the time I'd sorted it out, none of them wanted any cereal. I insisted. They grumped about it. I insisted. They grudgingly changed their minds.

Then there was a major disagreement about who'd get the Mr Men or Little Miss toy that was in the packet of Rice Crispies. It took me ten minutes to explain the notion of random good luck which goes as follows: if it falls into your bowl while you're pouring out your Crispies, then you're lucky and it's yours to keep. If it doesn't then you're unlucky and it isn't yours at all. In the end nobody got the toy when the Crispies were poured out, so I will have the pleasure of going through all this again another day.

Then, when they were finally chucking down cereal like it was the last pack in the world, the same cereal they didn't feel like having, I noticed they were taking turns putting their ears to each other's heads. When I enquired what they were up to, I was informed that they were listening to each other eat.

If I put bars on the windows and a turnstile on the front door, do you think it would entitle me to call the place a zoo?

*

I am sinking, literally, to new depths of homeliness and domesticity. Think about the ideal notion of a maternal figure and what do you see? Someone large and red-cheeked who huffs and puffs around the kitchen, fussing over the children, laughing raucously at silly jokes on the radio? Welcome to my world.

I have suddenly discovered why the image we carry around of the mother figure is one of such a large lady.

She's not large because she has had twenty children. Oh, no. It's because she finishes off the dinner plates of the twenty children.

I like my own cooking so much that I hate to see it go to waste. So when I can't get them to finish it off, guess what? Old JCB-mouth comes to the rescue and shovels it away into the vast and cavernous depths of his gut. No wonder that Japanese whaling ship came so close to shore last week when I went for a swim in the sea. I need to lose weight quickly or next time I might not be so lucky. I don't want to end up on a shelf in Super Crazy Prices in a John West tin.

I always finish my food first because the three of them never stop talking long enough to eat properly. I sit there drumming my fingers on the table thinking up new ways to get them to leave the table so I can dive into their grub. Shameful, isn't it?

I bet Naomi Campbell and Whackin' Cortez never carried on like this. I bet when they sat down to eat together once a year they divided the pea evenly between them and neither of them eyed up the other's half. And I bet they even left a little "manners piece" on the plate when they'd finished. Naomi probably got up from the table complaining about being stuffed and Whackin' probably wasn't able to dance for a week after such a feed.

Not me. I'm a three-helpings kind of guy. The first one is my starter, the second is my real dinner and the third is in lieu of my dessert which I never bother with because you have to draw the line somewhere. Then I start looking at the kids' plates.

Every time I open a cupboard now, I hear that music from Hitchcock's *Psycho*. In front of me is food, food, food: biscuits and cakes and tins of fruit and tins of salmon and tuna and beans and those little mini packs of sweets which I buy for the kids but which I end up eating all by myself, usually while I'm supposed to be tidying up. And when I go to my wardrobe looking for my Levis I swear

I can hear them shuffle away from the "These Still Fit Me" section down into the shadowy "Never To Be Worn Again" zone, just to escape the pain of having me squeeze into them.

I'm going to have to do a pilgrimage to Lough Derg or Croagh Patrick or something. I've tried the Scarsdale diet; it works, but it's Starvation-ville and you have to be in the right frame of mind for it (i.e. desperate). I've tried the BBC diet, too, but by the time I'd lost two stone on it we'd had three general elections and qualified for the World Cup twice.

Things came to a head this week when I was at a barbecue in a friend's garden. We were all sitting on these plastic bucket seats and mine kept sinking into the ground. New people joined us and they must have thought I worked in a circus because my chin barely touched the top of the table. That was embarrassing, so much so that it has set me on a course for Planet Thin. It will be a long and arduous voyage on which there will be many dangers and temptations, but with my silver boots and positive attitude I feel sure I will arrive there a lighter, wholer, happier Dad.

Now if I can just get the children to eat all their food...

*

I am in a state of shock. I actually made soup the other day which the children liked. It was a potato and leek soup and I served it up amid the usual groans and complaints that they didn't like it or that they weren't hungry or that vegetables have feelings too and it's cruel to cook them.

But there are times when every parent has to be firm, so I said grimly: "I will be really, really, really, *really* disappointed if you don't like this soup."

Lo and behold, they did like it. I couldn't get over it. Our children normally only like food depending on how quickly it can be cooked. If you go off and spend ten hours with your recipe books and then come back with something really fancy, they'll take a forkful and push the plate away; but if you make chips which take fifteen minutes they'll eat the plate. And if you go out for chips, which takes even less time, they'll not only eat the plates but they'll also promise to be good for a whole hour afterwards.

I haven't figured out a way of extending this theory to cover greens, so at the moment I'm using the old-fashioned method of withholding goodies and treats until all greens are eaten. Usually I end up feeling like a tyrant, but I want them to be healthy and to be able to see in the dark. It might come in handy if there's a power cut, you never know.

They don't realise it yet, but years from now when their complexions are really clear and boyfriends have to be beaten back from the front door – a job I have already reserved for myself – it'll be because of me and my insistence that they eat their greens. If the day ever comes when they get married, I'm going to refer to it in my speech.

"See the bride's complexion everybody? Pretty good, huh? You know why it's so good? I'll tell you: because I persevered when she was young. I suffered trying to get the kids to eat their greens."

And everybody will applaud and I'll feel really humble and glad that all the suffering was worthwhile.

I also made toffee the other day, which I know is kind of the other end of the spectrum. But Dads want to be loved, too. It can't all be about making them eat their greens and brush their teeth and tidy their rooms, you know?

So I made a huge slab of brown toffee. Yes, it's been a kitcheny kind of week. And I also made that boiled fruit cake I was talking about earlier. Indeed, I made it for the school fundraiser and they put a £5 price tag on it. I waited around for ages and ages to see who'd buy it because I wanted to follow them home and peep through their kitchen window when they were cutting it, but nobody bought it during the time I was there. I asked questions of everyone who was at the sale but nobody knew who bought my cake. So I had to go and bake another one just to see what it tasted like. Result? DEEEEELICIOUSSSSS!

As for the toffee, well, I've had to stop making it. No kidding. It was from a Delia Smith recipe, dead simple to make: just take two lorry loads of sugar, one E.U. regulation-sized mountain of butter and bubble for twenty minutes. Numbers One, Two and Three had it eaten in about twenty seconds flat after it had cooled, so I made some more and the same fate befell it. Now she-who-must-be-in-bed-by-ten has asked me not to make any more on the basis that toffee is cheap, but dentists are expensive. Duh! Why didn't I think of that?

The children are begging me to ignore this prohibition and I can feel my toffee-making hand itching every now and again. I need to deal with this addiction myself. I may have to join Toffeemakers Anonymous.

"Good evening. My name is Kevin, I'm a toffee-maker..."

To make amends I have decided that I am going to make some brown bread. There's nothing like a bit of wholesome roughage to make you feel pure again. Then, when I've had about as much purity as I can take, I'm going to make some more of that scrummy toffee.

*

I'm gumming for a Rolo. Or anything sweet, for that matter. We've had our first sweet-free week. We've never done this before and I wasn't sure how it was going to work. I knew the kids were going to get through it because I had the key to the sweetie cupboard, but how was I going to get through this mad, week-long experiment? Who was going to police the policeman?

Well, I made it alright, but not before I experienced serious sugar-free hell. In weak moments I could feel myself being drawn by some irresistible and invisible force into the kitchen. The next thing I'd snap out of it and there I'd be with my face pressed up against the door of the sweetie cupboard trying to wish the sweets out through solid wood.

Other times, I'd start hallucinating. I'd be at the butcher's or the dry cleaner's having a chat about some issue of world importance when Twix and Snickers bars would appear before my eyes. I'm certain the townsfolk thought I was going off the deep end. Next time you see someone muttering to himself and swatting away imaginary packets of M&Ms and Toffos and the like, try a little understanding – I was that swatter last week and, who knows, some day it could be you.

Irony of ironies, the children, who were the ones the sweet-free week was designed to help most, didn't have a problem with it. In fact, not one of them asked for sweets during the whole period. I have learned something deep and meaningful here about the sweet-buying habit in our house. Maybe, just maybe, I have discovered a whole new meaning to the phrase "sugar daddy". But I should be grateful for small mercies. So far my secret affair with all things chocolate hasn't taken away from my lithe, fit appearance and my stunning good looks.

Number Three came closest to breaking the communal iron will of the household on sweets because two of her boyfriends had birthday parties during the week. But even she, at four years of age, which in my book is pretty cool, confined herself to fairy cakes, crisps, popcorn, coca cola, ice cream, jelly, birthday cake, more jelly, more ice cream and fruit. Not one single sweet passed those lips of hers.

As is the ritual with most parties, the whole morning

is spent asking me if it's time to go yet. And then when we pile into the car to go to the blooming thing, she falls asleep. Parents will know this phenomenon. It leads to Grumpy Child Syndrome. Which means that when you get to the party and manage to bring the child around, you have to stay with the child for an hour before she has woken up enough to realise that parties can be fun. Meanwhile, the twenty things you were going to be able to do while the kid was at the party have become ten and are dwindling.

As a family we have devised a unique solution to this problem. We roll down all the windows in the car and start singing at the tops of our voices. The words of the song are very repetitive but they do the trick just fine. To the tune of "Glory, Glory Hallelujah", we sing: "Wakey, wakey, wakey, waaaakey!" And so it came to pass last week that the youngest was brought back to consciousness in time to bounce out of the car and party like crazy.

On the way back from delivering her, the kiddy tape was playing. I should point out that the kiddy tape is always playing in the car. My children put it on before their seat belts. I have listened to "Jake the Peg", "My Boomerang Won't Come Back" and "I've Lost My Mammy" until I am blue in the face. I cannot put the car in first gear unless that tape is playing. But last week I saw a glimmer of hope. "Davy Crockett" was playing, a song I'm sure everybody knows. It had just come to that memorable line, "He kilt him a bar when he wus only three", when Number One said with all seriousness: "Dad, he's getting tired singing that song, you can tell by his voice he's getting tired."

"Yes," I thought to myself as I stifled the urge to celebrate out loud, "there is a God."

*

My life flashed before my eyes the other day. But before

I go into that, let me make one thing absolutely clear: I do not spend my time watching daytime TV programmes. Occasionally, very occasionally, I might take a break to boil the kettle and have a cup of tea. And occasionally, very occasionally, I might wander into the sitting room while the kettle is boiling. And occasionally, very occasionally, I might turn on the TV just to see what's going on in the outside world. But that's the extent of it, honest, swear to God, cross my heart and hope to die.

So, given the minuscule amount of time I watch TV in the mornings, can you imagine my surprise when I turned on Richard and Judy's "This Morning" programme and saw that they were playing my tune?

All the daytime talk shows, not that I'd know much about that kind of thing, seem to be following Jerry Springer now. Everybody slags him off and yet his idea of putting the theme of each show in the bottom corner of the screen is all the rage. You know, like "By day he's a man, by night he's a woman" or "He hits you, why do you stay?" or "My sister and I share the same man" or, a particularly interesting one (I'm told), "Dumped while pregnant". We're talking serious class here.

So what are Richard and Judy doing this particular morning when I just happen by chance to turn on the telly? Nothing less than having their own, polished-up version of a Springer show. And the theme? "I married a corker, but now he's a porker."

It was riveting, so much so that I stayed watching it longer than my allotted twenty seconds. We heard about the guy who was like a whippet when he got married and now he's eating twelve doughnuts every evening on the way home from work because he's so hungry that he can't wait for his dinner. He can barely get into his car because he's so big. And then there was the guy who was like Michael Flatley when he got married; now he travels a lot because of his job and eats takeaways and drinks pints of beer to beat the band. The guy has gone from pork to porker to porkest.

I was watching all this and had a vague niggling feeling that it was all somehow familiar, but I just couldn't put my finger on it. And then, halfway through my second slice of apple tart, it hit me. I knew someone like that. I knew someone who started out on the great matrimonial version of Disneyland's Space Mountain as the thinnest of the thin. Now the poor bugger is all belly and looks like a pink pear on the beach. Mr Blobby without the spots. He's bald too, this guy, so he's got a head on him like I don't know what. But I couldn't remember his name. Imagine, he was in school with me and I couldn't remember his name? And then lightning struck.

The guy I was trying to remember was more or less the same height as me. With more or less the same shape as me. With more or less the same...! Oh, no! If he was, you know, er, large, and if he was the same as me, then that meant that I was, er, big for my age too!

Then and there, and Richard and Judy have to be thanked for this, I resolved to change my ways. I'm going back to Corkerville 'cos I've been away a long time. None of your NuTron diets for me boys and gals, I'm doing it cold turkey. If you want a name for it, call it the Ion Diet 'cos it's the diet I on.

To be very serious for a moment, this is going to mean job losses at Cadbury's, Jacobs, Bolands, Gateaux, HB and Tayto. But, look, I can't be responsible for everybody, can I? Besides, for every man like me who wises up, there're ten more to take my place on the great conveyor belt of consumerism.

The moral of this tale? Never knock daytime TV. That show was a moment of enlightenment for me. I suppose you could say it was a near-religious experience. At that very instant, profound words came to mind. They were the words of Vanessa during her show "Walk away, he's someone else's man" when she said that you've got to believe in yourself, have pride, reach high and don't sell yourself short. Yes indeed, keep your eyes on the golden horizon of new tomorrows. Hallelujah.

*

I will begin today with, let me see now, the Smarties egg. Or will I have the Black Magic egg? No, maybe not. Dark chocolate first thing is only something a really unsophisticated person would indulge in. Perhaps I'll avoid both of them and go for the Quality Street egg. You can't go wrong with Quality Street. You always know where you are with Quality Street. I swear by them, personally.

You see, pacing yourself is the key to Easter Sunday. You wouldn't want to be eating too many chocolate eggs before dinner time. That's why I'm having only one for breakfast, one for elevenses, and then one immediately after dinner. Then I'll have one for the afternoonses, one right after tea, and one while I'm watching the movie on the box tonight. Moderation in all things, that's what I say, especially when it comes to moderation.

Earlier this week those demented, high energy persons we laughingly refer to as our children and I painted some hard-boiled eggs. That was fun. The dining room table now has a kind of yellowish, brownish, bluish, reddish tinge through it. The box of paints said they would wash off with water. They didn't wash off with water. I may have to sue.

The eggs, on the other hand, look delightful. All multicoloured and Eastery. It is the best way of keeping the children occupied for thirty minutes, provided you don't mind spending thirty minutes beforehand rooting out all the paint, the brushes, and the newspapers to work on, and rolling up all the sleeves and finding paper to paint on, and then spending thirty minutes afterwards clearing everything away and washing the paint off the brushes and the paint pots. Apart from that, it's really ideal. She-who-can jump-over-her-own-height-backwards thought so, too.

"It must have killed the afternoon nicely for you," she said all breezy and bright.

"Never mind the afternoon," I said, "it nearly killed me."

And speaking of being killed, I was attacked by a dog the other day. No kidding. I was out with Number Three in her buggy delivering flyers for a fund-raising event and this big b*****d of a collie dog made a run at me. He bit a hole in the backside of my cool Russell Athletic (Established USA 1982 by Benjamin Russell) training pants. Then he made a second run at me but luckily I was screaming and crying so much that I frightened him off. Thank God for fear – but I dread to think of the effect it had on the four-year-old who was watching all this. She's probably going to have a phobia about dogs too. The gas of it was that the owner was standing four feet away and she was too gobsmacked to do anything about it. Obviously, this was the first time Lassie chose to savage a human while she was watching.

Which brings me to my favourite subject. The owners of dogs that are taller than my knee have two birth defects. They have no brain and they have no eyes. I know they have no brain because of the way they do not realise that little Woofy could possibly rip a hole in your body. And if he ever did, you can bet your tetanus injection it was just for play.

And they have no eyes either, because when Woofy does a woopsie on the path where we have to walk or on the grass in the park where we sit or where the children play, the owners simply do not see it or understand the ugliness of it. Stick the dog's nose in it? Don't waste your time. Stick the owner's nose in it instead.

Now, where was I? Oh, yes, the collie who bit a hole in my cool pants. The point I wanted to make was that the only reason I was there was because I was doing voluntary work. I, being of sound mind and body, was out supporting a fund-raising event, on my own time and for no money. I never realised that by staying at home full time I'd be a sitting duck for voluntary work. Okay, call me naïve if you want to, but I really didn't twig this until it was too late. So, there I am, out one afternoon doing God's work when I get attacked by a collie with an attitude problem. The moral of the story? Help nobody. Let them raise money some other way, on somebody else's time.

Now, where are those eggs? Ranting like this always gives me an appetite.

*

The eating habits of my children have gone to the dogs. Every day of the week I have a different dish for them, but each of the kids now hates at least one of them. I am now surrounded by cookery books, trying to devise new menus and dishes which will be acceptable to them. I'd let them choose the menu themselves, only chicken nuggets and HB Viennetta every day is not what I call a varied diet.

Last week I found myself cooking spaghetti with a meat sauce and it had to be presented in four separate bowls for serving. Number One likes the pasta and the meat but doesn't like the tomato sauce. Number Two likes the pasta and the tomato sauce but doesn't like the meat. Number Three likes the pasta and doesn't like the meat or the tomato sauce.

It's getting like this for nearly every meal now. When one hears that the other doesn't like some part of the dinner, then she picks another part of the dinner to hate, just to be different. There is no way of getting them to eat if they don't want to. And I refuse to take them to McDonalds, because too much of that food just leaves them hungrier than ever. And I have to work more 'cos it costs a lot.

In fact, I blame McDonalds for the poor eating habits of my kids. They like the stuff so much that they now measure everything else against it. I'm trying to introduce cabbage to the menu. Have you any idea how difficult that is to achieve with kids who think the highest form of food is a beef patty?

"What is that?" Number Two asked in a tone which suggested I was about to be knifed.

"It's cabbage," I said.

"Cabbage? What's cabbage?"

"It's just like broccoli."

"Broccoli is like trees, this isn't."

"This is broccoli before it gets to be like trees."

"And what's that smell?"

"That's the cabbage smell, isn't it lovely?"

"It's disgusting. Do I have to eat this?"

"That would please me, yes."

"Can I leave the table? I think I'm going to be sick."

When my children are much, much older, they will realise how much work goes into cooking a meal. When they don't like something, they'll be much more diplomatic about it. Like in about twenty years' time. In the meantime, it's back to the drawing board.

Speaking of the drawing board... I had an arrangement with the neighbour that I would drop her kids and my kids to an outing and she would collect her own afterwards. Up to now I have lived with the guilt of forgetting to pick up my children at various places. Once, in an unforgettable lapse of memory, I forgot to pick up somebody else's child, something the parents of the child have probably never really forgiven me for. But I'm getting sidetracked here.

I always thought that this forgetting thing was an exclusively male preserve, on the basis that we men are always preoccupied with serious issues, like the melting ice cap or the threat of nuclear war or the price of CDs.

But, no. Lo and behold, the female neighbour forgot to collect her child. Admittedly, there was work pressure involved, but the fact is that she did forget. What a relief: I thought it was just me. I was celebrating for ages with nothing but champagne, until some of the stuffy neighbours began to complain about the empties in their gardens and I had to cool it and get back to normal life again.

Normal life in our house means keeping the children amused all the time. Usually this involves taking them out somewhere, but if that somewhere is not to their liking, then you had better watch out because they all get mysterious pains and illnesses. If we go for a walk, they get pains in their ankles or in their tummies, or a stitch in their sides. If the drive is too long, they get sick in their tummies and sometimes the car. If the place is not interesting enough, they get mysterious headaches. If the sun is too hot, we have to buy drinks because they're thirsty. Often they can't go anywhere because they need to do a pee first.

What I'm thinking of doing is making a tape recording of their moaning: "I've a headache, I'm thirsty, I'm tired, I've a pain in my tummy, I'm feeling sick, I'm bored." And if they misbehave, then they're going to have to listen to it for a change.

*

I was making Irish stew the other day. In the sitting room the deafening sounds of *Grease* bounced off the walls as the three of them practised their John Travolta moves. Number One broke off being Sandy to wander in and ask what I was doing. When I told her, she rewarded my efforts in true '50s American cheerleader fashion with a resounding: "Yeeuch." As I think I have noted on many occasions in the past, if it's not made of chocolate, sugar or ice cream, my children consider it bad food. But I will persevere. They need old-fashioned things like protein, minerals, vitamins and iron. And they will get them, whether they like it or not.

My only concession to totally sweetie-free food is my recent pattern of making apple tarts and meringues, both allowed on my diet. I have been following Delia Smith to the letter in these two endeavours. She is a goddess. If it were biologically possible, I would have her children. I know I should be supporting Darina Allen but, don't get me wrong, it's nothing personal. It's like going to a disco. Delia's the first girl I danced with and I liked her so much I've stuck with her.

Anyway, she-who-puts-bread-on-our-table decided in her wisdom that she'd buy me a cookery book – just to help along the creative juices I've been letting flow in the kitchen. I am not too proud to admit that new books on cooking are always welcome. So, naturally, when she bought it I asked with barely concealed excitement which book she'd chosen.

"It's fairly simple," she said biting her lip, no doubt holding back the urge to add, "like you."

"Oh, I see. You mean it's like 'How to be a Better Cook'," I said, chuckling at my fabulous wit.

"No, it's more basic than that," she said with ne'er a hint of humour.

"Oh?"

And so it is. Delia Smith really does have a book called "How to Cook" and it is now my constant companion. I am going to learn from this book. I am going to become a better cook, a better father, a better person in the world. I am also going to make things the children will eat. Put simply, I am going to excel.

An area where I am not excelling at the moment is that of fridge management. This is an area of domesticity for which I have had absolutely no training and so I must rely on what I can only humorously refer to as my "instincts". These same instincts in turn rely heavily on my sense of smell. In other words, when something smells bad in the fridge, I hunt it down mercilessly until I have found it and then exact a terrible revenge by dumping it unceremoniously in the bin.

However, my abilities in fridge management and those of she-who-thinks-Frasier-is-better-looking-than-I-am are not one and the same. This has led to zones of itsy-bitsy tetchiness between us. There was the time I overlooked six slices of gorgeous cooked ham while fretting about what to give the children for lunch. And the time her favourite pâté was left to acquire an attractive green fringe of mould. And the time I forgot the cucumber in the bottom drawer and we had to fish it out weeks later with a soup spoon. These things were meant to try us – except that I have been tried and found guilty of wanton neglect of the white kitchen appliance which keeps food fresh.

But then it's easy to criticise when you're on the outside looking in, isn't it? It's a whole different enchilada when you're trying to run a house, raise a family, and manage the contents of a fridge at the same time.

As if that wasn't enough, Goldie, our hip-hop goldfish, has taken a turn. He's been swimming upside down for days and we suspect it is something in the water. I'm no fish expert, but he looks to me like he needs a chiropractor to snap him back into shape again. I hope he pulls through; I just couldn't go through the trauma of a fish funeral right now.

This is not to say the week hasn't had its high points. One was Number Two's delight at getting her uniform from Brownies. To think that she'll be having her first powwow soon. I'm dying to find out how to roll a neckerchief correctly and how to wear a woggle in the way a woggle must be worn. All together now: "Ging gang gully gully..."

Chapter Three

School days are the happiest days of their lives because they have their own private taxi

It's time to cover the books and kiss goodbye the lie-ins. Another school year beckons and the season of routine and timetables is upon us. Number Three starts "big school" tomorrow. It is the end of an era. If I thought that taking the stabilisers off her bike earlier this month was bad, this has to be worse. Will they let me sit in the class with her? Can I be there at break-time? If she doesn't know the answer to something, can I answer it? Such are the crazed thoughts of a sentimental parent. I am comforted, however, by the knowledge that her best pal is starting with her and she'll have her two sisters in the higher classes, so she won't be lonely.

The teachers should have fun teaching this one. She asked me the other day what animal we get water from. I was about to tell her it was an animal called The Corporation, but smart answers like that tend to confuse rather than enlighten. Another day recently she had been hungry and grumpy. I asked her if she'd wash her hands before sitting down to eat and she threw a wobbly.

"I don't want to wash my hands."

"You have to wash your hands before you eat your food."

"I don't want to."

"You have to."

"Dad, you're not the boss."

"I am the boss. I'm your Dad, so I'm the boss."

"God is the boss, not you."

"That's true, but if God was here right now I know for a fact that He'd like you to wash your hands."

Shheeesh. That's just one example of negotiations with one child at one point in the day. Multiply by seven or eight and then by three to get a true measure of what summer living is like when the kids are on holidays.

Still, the thing I will miss most when they are back in school will be the easy-going lifestyle. Feeding them whenever they were hungry. Getting them to bed about five minutes before it was time for me to flop. The noise about the place. The constant games that have rules that change all the time. The sheer high-pitched velocity of their play. Oh, and not having to be up at seven in the morning.

However, there are things I will look forward to as well. These include the peace and quiet in the mornings once I've dropped them in, the ability to think straight and plan out my days, the order and the routine (even though I'll hate it at first), and the fact that the weekends will feel like weekends again.

Needless to say, all these positives will be more or less neutralised by having to run a taxi service for them in the afternoons, but you can't have everything. If God had wanted us to have an easy life, He would have put self-cleaning surfaces on everything.

And if He had wanted me in particular to have a really easy life, He would have given me children who were a little less fond of giving me a hard time. I have referred to my decision to go on a diet once the summer is over. Part of the reason is that I eat the children's food as well as my own. When you work in an office you don't have this kind of temptation. Pull that stunt in the canteen and you can kiss goodbye to your career prospects.

I have tried to stop, but it's no use. I cook really nice food and I hate to see it going to waste. You could almost say I am a regular Italian momma, big, bustling around the kitchen, mumbling a language to myself that nobody else understands, tasting everything to make sure it's cooked properly, and swinging between flying off the handle and hugging and kissing the children to death. Our house is a proper little dramatic opera sometimes.

But all that pales into insignificance compared with the song Numbers Two and Three were singing the other day. They always use the tune from the gas ad, the one with the three bears singing "Fifty-Fifty Cashback", and put their own words to it. This particular day they were singing: "Our Dad's got big boobies" to this same tune. It was hurtful and cruel and they laughed like drunken hyenas when they saw I was listening. The little rats.

So that's it. Enough is enough. No more will I suffer the slings and arrows of outrageous children. Pass the phone book, it's time to talk the talk and walk the walk.

*

I think I whinged too much about the kids being off all summer. You never appreciate what you have until it's gone. Now they're back to school and something precious that I enjoyed day in and day out has been taken away from me. I want my lie-ins back. I hate having to get up at 7.15 every morning on the dot to get them in on time. It is a cruel and unusual punishment. Nobody said having kids was going to be like being in the Army. At least the Army pays for your clothes.

And the lunches! Just when you think it's safe to sit down and watch a bit of telly in the evening, the L word rears its head. Lunches have to be made the night before in our house, otherwise Papa No-Hair here gets a teensy-weensy bit stressed and tetchy in the mornings. Somebody should start up a dial-a-school-lunch delivery service, just like the pizza people.

Speaking of unusual punishment, mine all like peanut butter sandwiches, but every time I open the peanut butter jar I feel faint from the smell of it. When I'm making the sandwiches, she-who-does-the-breadwinning stands beside me swabbing my forehead with a damp cloth – a bit like "ER" during an emergency operation.

And speaking of emergencies, I tried the new Bloomfields supermarket recently. Getting to it through the traffic in Dun Laoghaire nearly gave me a heart attack. Then when I got there, another layer of pressure was added.

My lot are crèche addicts for some reason. Once they hear the word "crèche" they want to go to it. Bloomfields has one, which costs £4 per hour for three children.

I did the shopping by running around the store and piling up the trolley, to get through the checkout and dash back to the crèche in under an hour so I would not have to pay double. I made it with just seconds to go before I was into the second hour. Now I know how Frankie Fredericks felt when he beat Donovan Bailey in the 100 metres. I danced around, punched the air, took the applause and then felt a surge of pride as the three of them were marched out to me. Then I got a serious indigestion pain and had to go home and lie down.

Shopping was never meant to be this way. I'd stood at the bleaches and cleaners section and was hit by the very thing you don't want to be hit with when you're under time pressure: indecision. Was it going to be the Jif Kitchen gun with free Ballerina Cloth? Or the Flash Mildew with boosted bleach? Or the Dettox with anti-bacterial mould remover? Or Dr Beckman's Hob Cleaner (first aid for hobs)? In the end I bought none of them because I couldn't make up my mind.

At the Great Wall of China, otherwise known as the cereals section, it was the same thing. I couldn't find the Weetaflakes because all the boxes look so alike. Then I lost my place while I was changing a small Alpen muesli for a big Alpen muesli and had to start all over again. It got so stressful I could feel the urge to go to the toilet coming on and had to leave without the Weetaflakes, which goes to prove that Weetaflakes can keep you regular even if you don't eat them.

But this is all part of the great tapestry of life when the kids go back to school. You expect this kind of thing. What you don't expect are the sudden shocks. No sooner had I set into my first serious pot scrubbing since the holidays when I noticed water in one of my black Marigolds. Distraught, I filled it with water and found it was leaking like the government before Budget day. This was my first pair of black Marigolds. They were with me from the start, right from when this whole househusbanding adventure began. They were part of the family. They will be irreplaceable. Until I buy another pair.

Quote of the Week: "You're not born yet."
> – Number Two telling Number Three why she can't play baby in the game of Mums and Dads.

*

It's time to dust off the old taxi sign and stick it on top of the car. Yup, now that they are back at school it's extra-curricular activities time again. The untrained monkeys that my wife tries to convince me are my children are being lined up for all sorts of extra classes and courses that I cannot afford. The lack of money is apparently a minor detail to be ignored if they are to have an interesting and fulfilling childhood.

This weekend is being dedicated to just one job: drawing up a chart listing where the children have to be on each day of the week, at what time and in what clothes. My life, or what's left of it, will be hell without this chart. It is not unknown for me to forget one of them at one place or another, or bring one to ballet with her swimming togs, or turn up at drama on piano day.

To say I am blue in the face from buying ballet pumps, gym shoes, finding a new piano teacher, checking out gym classes, French classes, yogic flying, car maintenance, and make-your-own-Mir-space-station classes, is putting it mildly.

And when I eventually have them all set up with their special activities, the pace of life is going to shift up into an even higher gear. Every weekday will be a Hollywood production, with exciting location changes, fabulous costumes, endless travel, and nail-biting thrills. I'll have a minor but important role as the sweaty, surly taxi driver.

This lifestyle, as you may have gathered, leaves precious little time for other things, like meal times and homework and odd moments when we exchange civil discourse. We'll have to make a really special effort to find time for those.

When we're up and running, I'm going to be so tired that I will spend Saturdays and Sundays hibernating in a special soundproof room with the windows blackened out. Then, come Monday morning, I'll pop a few painkillers and start the whole thing all over again. It's a bit like a condensed version of the lifestyle of the North American brown bear, except it happens week in, week out and, of course, bears don't know about painkillers yet.

Speaking of bears, Number Two had a nightmare the other night and refused point blank to sleep in her bed on her own. Reasoning doesn't work at that hour of the morning, so I had to clamber in. It was like Daddy bear sleeping in Baby bear's bed, with Baby bear still in it. I couldn't get to sleep for ages because of the sound she makes sucking her thumb. When I woke up the next morning I had the most excruciating pain in my already fragile neck. I was thumping the pillow, making a mental note to burn it and buy another when I suddenly got an excruciating pain in my hand too. I'd hit the torch she keeps under the pillow I'd just slept on all night.

So, is there any joy, I hear you ask? Why, yes, now

that you mention it. I have rediscovered the joys of keepyups and heading. For those of you who are baffled, keepyups is the art of keeping a football off the ground with your feet and heading is when you do it with your head. I know you can achieve the same end result by just holding the ball in your hands, but there's not much challenge in that, is there?

The neighbour's son counted me up to 50 with keepyups the other day and went away mightily impressed. I have to say I was impressed myself, or at least I was after I'd had a long lie down on the couch. The only problem now is that I think I might have sent the wrong signal out to the neighbourhood. I can see all sorts of kids coming around to try and beat my total. I dread the day when I have to compete with a ten-year-old Ryan Giggs while my three girls look on. It's getting so I can't sleep at night. Somewhere out there is a kid who's faster, meaner, and leaner than I am. And he's got a ball with my name on it.

*

What in the name of God was I doing? Admittedly, it was the first week of extra-curricular activities for the kids. Things were hectic. A whole new routine and timetable was about to roll out. But that's no excuse. Either I'm going to do this househusbanding thing properly or I might as well not do it at all.

Number One was all lined up to go back to her piano lessons. The thing was, her piano teacher had moved, so we were to drive to the new house. When we arrived it was raining. The other two were murdering each other in the back of the steamed-up car. And the piano teacher wasn't home.

So we went for a drive to the shops and picked up a few bits and pieces and then we called back. The piano teacher still wasn't home. Then I found a phone and called her, but the number I had was wrong and I had to try dialling different combinations of the seven-digit number. The phrase "on a loser" kept going around in my head.

So we went home. I was cheesed off. Number One was delighted because it meant no piano practise for another week, but fortunately she kept her glee to herself. Me, I was rehearsing my strategy for the next phone conversation with the piano teacher. Would I be "indignant parent", taking the high moral tone, complaining about the time wasted and the stress of driving through heavy traffic; or would I be "sympathetic but cute parent", understanding her situation, could have happened to a bishop, we all make mistakes, any chance of a free lesson to make up for it? At teatime the phone rang.

"Was our lesson for half-two or half-four today?" she asked.

"Half-two," I said, ready to pounce, "but you weren't there."

"Oh, yes, I was. I was in all afternoon waiting for you."

"We called at half-two, waited quarter of an hour, went away, came back and you still weren't there," I said, feeling like I was winning this one.

"But did you not see the car parked in front of the door?"

"There was no car there," I said.

"What house were you at?"

"At your house, number seventy-five."

"I live in number seventy-nine."

"Oh."

This was in the same week that I had a major summit negotiation with the same child about getting her ears pierced. It's a personal thing; I don't like piercing. Anything that involves putting a needle through the skin is out with me. I know in my heart that if it starts at the ears when she's nine, it'll be the bellybutton by the time she's thirteen, the eyebrows when she's sixteen and the tongue when she's nineteen. Then she'll marry a tattoo artist, open a little shop that smells of Indian oil and incense, live from hand to mouth, get into drugs, get busted trying to smuggle heroin out of Pakistan, and spend the best years of her life sharing a cell and one potty with fifty women. As a parent I feel responsible to guide her away from all that.

I told her that at sixteen she may have her ears pierced. No, she cried, because she does acting classes and they teach her to do this. No, she said, DeeDee down the road is my age and she has her ears pierced. No way, I replied, I'm not allowing it. So we went through the "whys", which included ear infection and very little else, if the truth be known. But this gal is going to be a horse trader. Okay, she said, how about when I'm eleven. No way, I said, and we haggled, eventually settling on thirteen.

In the old days, if a father said something, that was it. Now it's parenting by negotiation and I had to get three union officials in for the children.

Finally, get me the silver boots and strap a ray gun to me, I am now NuTron Man. Yes, I have gone the way of countless thousands and embraced the NuTron diet. They asked me at the NuTron shop why I wanted to lose weight and I told them it was for health reasons. That caused a few suppressed giggles.

"Nothing to do with you being overweight then," one of the ladies enquired diplomatically.

"Well, yeah, okay, just a little," I replied meekly.

Now, armed with my red list of must-not-eats and my green list of must-eats, I am ready to face a bold new future. The thought of all those trousers I'll get to wear again is bringing a sentimental tear to my eye. It won't be much longer now, old buddies.

*

I don't know what they're teaching kids in school these days. The seven-year-old came home the other day after the Archbishop had visited her class. They'd had a big talk on the passage in the Bible about us being the sheep who needed minding and all that. She'd found it very enjoyable and after a long, rambling description of the story, she asked me if I knew that Jesus was our sheepdog.

"Our what?" I asked, wondering if I'd heard it right.

"Jesus is our sheepdog," she said. "He looks after us and if we go off into another field he comes after us and brings us back to the right field."

Obviously, if she thought Jesus was now Shep the Sheepdog, there'd been a slight misinterpretation here. I let it go for a while and then later on brought up the subject again, gently. When she found out that he was our shepherd she seemed a little put out but had to agree it made much more sense, even if it wasn't half as interesting. As I was going through all this, Number Three wandered in, in a distressed state. I asked her what the problem was and, barely able to contain her grief, she said she couldn't find her saveline.

"Your what?" I asked, wondering if I'd heard it right.

"My saveline," she repeated as if I was deaf or stupid or both, "my lips're sore."

The makers of Vaseline probably don't know this but their product has suddenly become the height of cool with our Number Three. She doesn't give a toss about the fact that everybody else runs a mile in case she tries to kiss them with petroleum jelly smeared all over her mouth. Needless to say, we found her "Saveline" in her trouser pocket, exactly where she'd left it.

Then Number Two came along and informed me that she and Number One were going to learn how to say their names in burp language.

"You what?" I asked, again wondering if I'd heard right.

"Burp language," she repeated proudly. "Our friend Andrew is able to do it and so is John. It's cool."

In case you don't know what I can look forward to as my children learn to say their names in burp language, let me explain. I have seen it take place in other households. It will consist of my daughters belching around the house like lumberjacks on a pub crawl from one end of the day to the other. And when this feat has reached its natural state of perfection, because practise makes it that way, they will then perform it in front of my face. I will quickly suss that it sounds only vaguely like their names but because I am a caring adult I will clap wildly and enthusiastically at their magnificent achievement.

I hope to Shep they forget about this plan before it ever gets off the ground.

*

What is it that makes me do these things? They were looking for parent volunteers to go on a school trip and before I knew it my hand was in the air. I looked at my raised arm with a mixture of disappointment and disgust. I wanted to disown it then and there but I've been attached to it since birth and, hell, maybe it wouldn't be so bad after all.

I was wrong.

It was worse than bad. It was hell on earth. Our little catchphrase for the day was "twenty-two go to the zoo". That's twenty-two six-year-olds, in case you didn't know. And I was one of five or so parents who, along with the teacher, were going along for the ride of our lives. On the positive side, it was good training should I ever decide to join the riot police.

My car had five children, including one of my own. The journey took only half an hour but it was as long as my eardrums could hold out. If it was an Olympic event, these children could laugh and shout for Ireland. By the time we got there I was actually looking forward to going into the monkey house for a bit of peace and quiet.

As it turned out, we didn't stay there long enough to even see all the monkeys. Being my first time at this kind of thing, I didn't realise that this was to be a trip to the Zoo at speed. The gang of twenty-two charged from the front gate down to see the ducks, then they charged up to see the monkey house. Then they raced to the bird house, then the lemurs, then pets corner, then the reptile house. By the time we got to the bat house we'd only been ten minutes in the place and I was badly in need of St John's Ambulance, which I discovered isn't on duty during the week. Have you ever heard twenty-two children spooking themselves out in the bat house shouting: "wooooo, wooooo!"?

We had a snack at the playground then and, boy, did we need it. Ever see Vietnam movies where the soldiers at the front line just kind of stare into space during a break in the fighting? Well, that was us adults. We did use the time to regroup and reorganise, though. Myself and Alison, whose two boys were on the trip, were sent up to ride point. Nobody was to run ahead of us and we were to lead the way.

Once fed, watered and rested, the charging herd were off again. Our new system worked well until we passed a playground and suddenly found there was no-one behind us any more. But once we got into it again, we were fine. We trotted passed the camels, flew passed the elephants, and only stopped long enough at the hippo to fling apples into his pool.

Then the gang all ran for the swings beside the hippo, so we had to run after them. There I developed enormous biceps from the weight of four rucksacks on one arm and from pushing a continuous queue of children on the swings with the other.

After that it was the polar bears, the seals, the lions, the gorilla and then the gibbons. And as if the pace of the thing wasn't bad enough, the sun came out and fried us all, so they all had to take off their coats and jumpers. I looked like Johnny Fortycoats by the time we were through.

At the end of this three-hour zoological assault course we headed for the cars. The other parents were discussing which was the best route to take home through lunchtime traffic, but I couldn't hear a word because I'd already put the cotton wool in my ears. They should have a special educational programme for parents where they teach us to "Just Say No!" when we're tempted to go on these trips.

Speaking of education, Number One came home from school the other day with a fascinating insight into cultural habits in China. It turns out her pal Stephen, an authority on Chinese history and customs, had some startling information. When a man dies in China, the wife cuts off his willy and wears it around her neck. I was about to say that in America they do it when the man is sleeping, but I knew that would only confuse her more. You would not believe the job I had convincing her that this is not a Chinese custom. She thought I was the one who was kidding.

*

The first back-to-school bug has hit the house. Number Three came down with something or other and had a temperature for five days. It's been so much fun I found myself flicking through travel brochures in free moments.

Most of the week the youngest one was only fit to lie on the couch and watch cartoons or videos. That worked fine until the video machine broke down on Wednesday. Then I had to find a same-day repair shop so that the child didn't have to suffer her way through "Kilroy" and "Richard and Judy" in the mornings and "Countdown" and "Fifteen to One" in the afternoons.

Except the same-day repair shop only did what it said it would do if you dropped your broken machine in before ten in the morning. So we agreed it would be ready the following day, in the morning. The following day I rang and was told, no, it wouldn't be ready. Your man couldn't find a gidgetywizchop that fits over the wurbalygrungetit.

I repeated his firm's claim in the Yellow Pages that it was a same-day repair service but I think this just upset the poor man. We haggled until we agreed I'd ring at four in the afternoon.

Then I had the unsavoury task, for the second time that week, of getting a urine sample from Number Three. She thought this was the weirdest thing she'd ever seen – me holding one of those impossibly small plastic jars under her wee as she did her business. It wasn't exactly a bag of laughs for me either. That stuff is scalding hot when it comes out. I never had to do anything like that when I worked in an office.

I rang the video repair shop an hour early at three and, lo, the machine was ready. Off I went in the pouring rain with three children in a steamy car, one of whom was spewing virally infected carbon dioxide all over the place, and with one plastic jar of fresh widdle in my pocket. I parked and ran through the rain to the shop, only to find out that the repair service works out of a different shop. This meant a further four hundred yard dash through the teeming rain.

Would the car be clamped? Would the children be stolen? Would the other two get infected with Number Three's bug? Would the video get soaked on the way back and never work again? Would it cost me a fortune? Would the widdle leak in my pocket? Would I ever reach old age? Such are the thoughts of a pressured househusband.

But everything turned out fine. Not only did the vid work, and not cost me a fortune to get fixed, but I still had one more night on *Basil The Great Mouse Detective* and *Hercules*, which I'd borrowed from the Xtravision store. Yeeessss, there is a God! The same video store, incidentally, which once told me I owed £8 on *Good Will Hunting* because it was three days late. No way, I said, and luckily I could prove it. Phew! Always chat to the people behind the counters; that way they'll remember your baldy head and know you've been a good boy.

Video safe in the boot, we went on to the hospital with the wee sample. Number Three was not well and wanted to be in bed. Numbers One and Two still had their homework to do and were in an ugly mood over it. The traffic was crawling, it was still raining and I was trying to figure out what I'd cook for dinner in between bouts of wishing I'd been born as Michael Bolton. Maybe it's hair envy.

Our hospital was built when people rode bicycles because the car park only fits ten cars. The fact that I got a space meant I had to remember to buy a lottery ticket that night. I felt good. I deposited the sample, wished the nurse luck with it, and returned to my steamy car in particular and chaotic life in general. Then it was back home via the lottery shop to relative comfort, safety and sanity.

Things could have ended so well. I could have won the lottery. I could have been a new millionaire boring the backside off people about where I went skiing and who I met there and how the new Merc holds on the corners. But I didn't win the lottery, no sir, and then two days later, she-who-is-the-font-of-all-cutlinary-knowledge told me that, ooops, *Hercules* and *Basil* were still in her car and would I mind dropping them back.

*

Number Three has hit the wall. Three weeks or so into big school and she tells me she doesn't want to go. It's not so much that she doesn't want to go, it's more she doesn't want to get out of bed in the mornings to go. It's like she's tried it, she knows she can do it, now can we move on to something else, please? I knew this would happen.

"Why do I have to go to school?" she asked the other morning from under the covers.

"So that you can learn lots of things."

"But why?"

"So that when you grow up you can do really interesting things."

"Like what?"

"Like travel the world and meet interesting people and live in fabulous places."

I know I was overselling it but I was running late.

"I want to live in a castle when I grow up," came the muffled reply.

"Well, there you go. Out of bed quick so I can get you to school because the quicker you get to school, the quicker you get your castle."

"Oh, alright then."

I hope she forgets this conversation by the time she hits her twenties, just in case things don't work out exactly as planned.

And speaking of planning, I made a big effort to do my supermarket shopping without the children last week. I went to Dunnes of Cornelscourt and reckoned I'd fly around the place without having the three monkeys grabbing everything in sight and using the trolley as a go-kart. Leaving aside the fact that I couldn't get freezer bags, a cheese slicer, our favourite brand of peanut butter, or a mop head, it went smoothly enough.

Except at the checkout I didn't have a Dunnes loyalty card and I hate to lose valuable points. The nice girl gave me a new card and told me to hand in my application form at information. So off I went to information where there was a woman in line in front of me. She had a packet of bin liners which didn't fit her bin. The girl behind the counter was suitably concerned about this. I waited. They checked one of the bags. Everything seemed fine. Then two more supervisor types came over. They too inspected the bags. Now everybody was concerned, including myself because I know what it's like to clean out a kitchen bin that has no bag in it. So I waited some more and then looked at my watch. It was ten past twelve and I still had to go home, unload the shopping and collect Number Three at quarter to one. At last there was a solution.

"You need bigger bin liners," one of the supervisors said.

"Yeah, yeah, bigger ones," the other two muttered in agreement.

"But these are the large ones," said the poor confused woman with the unlined bin.

"Ah yes, but you have to get the Jumbo liners. They're the ones to fit your bin."

"You mean the large ones won't work?" she asked, getting it at last.

"No," said the supervisor, "the large ones only fit smaller bins."

I kid you not, that's what she said: "the large ones only fit smaller bins." I'm glad I stay at home because otherwise I'd miss lines like that. The large ones only fit smaller bins.

So what else? Oh, yes, I am baking my own bread now because of this NuTron diet. The children will not eat it. I am also cooking lots of stir-fries. The children will not eat them. I am also drinking four pints of water a day to clear out my system of toxins, which means I am peeing like a newborn at all hours of the day and night. I'm just short of keeping a potty with me at all times.

The good part is I get to go on this machine at the NuTron mothership which gives my stomach a serious electric tickle. The equivalent of fifty sit-ups, they tell me. It's going to get pretty damn embarrassing when strange women start falling for me, I can tell you.

While I was reading "Salmonella: Is Your Kitchen a Theme Park for Germs?" the other day, Number One sidled up and said: "Looking thin, Dad." Was I dreaming? Had I really heard that? Then it occurred to me. Of course. She must want something really, really, really big for Christmas. You can't start too early where Christmas is concerned. God bless her but, you know, I think flattery works a treat on me. I feel Santa will be generous this year.

*

The post-Christmas routine started for real again this week. We were back to doing two million things in the afternoons, on top of the usual homework. On Monday there's soccer and hockey; on Tuesday there's piano and Brownies; on Wednesday there's two separate ballet classes; and on Thursday there's French and a heavy homework load for Number Two. Friday is the only day that is clear in the afternoon. This is so they can either visit pals or have pals home for a play. If they are all out visiting, I go to the supermarket. If they have friends over to play, I hide in my room.

It's only January and I'm tired already. Why doesn't the summer hurry up and come? I want to laze around in the mornings. I want to goof off in the afternoons. I want to loll about in the evenings. Instead, what am I facing? An endless road to June, filled with extracurricular activities, even on Saturdays. On Saturday mornings we have swimming and drama now. Drama, no less. It's a long way from drama on Saturdays that I was reared, I can tell you.

Yet this is the kind of thing which fills up the school terms. Someone asked me the other day was there anything about being at home full time that I hadn't expected. I said I hadn't expected it to be so busy. It's busy all the time, during the day and during the night, right up to my bedtime.

I'm in bed at ten o'clock. I was never in bed before midnight when I was working in an office. The reason is that I'm so tired now. Even when we get invited out somewhere of an evening, we're first to leave because I'm looking at my watch and signalling to she-who-can-boogie-'til-dawn for us to go.

We went to a fortieth birthday party last weekend and we left at half past twelve. Because the party was over? No. Because we were blotto? No way. Because lil' ol' me was so bunched tired that I had to go home and go to sleep. Luckily I had brought the crowbar with me to prise the Boogie Queen's fingers off the doorways. It's quicker that way. But, I ask you, is this monastic work-filled existence any way for a self-respecting kind-of-youngish man to have to live?

This is what children do to you. They wear you out. They're great fun, but they wear you out. They and the work they create, which brings me back to my point. During school term it is one endless round of lunch making and dinner cooking, homework and piano practise, teeth brushing and hair combing, clothes washing and clothes drying. Makes you wonder why anyone in their right mind would want to do it, doesn't it? You don't have to answer that.

But then you reach a point, as I did the other night, when something happens that just puts everything in context. It was their bedtime. We'd had a Zen kind of evening when not a negative word was heard. There were no protests from Number Three when I asked her to get into her "jahmies". We did the teeth without a squeal or a single badly aimed spit. We chose clothes for the morning and my suggestions did not meet with a shower of complaints. Then we read the bedtime story.

It was a story about a cat, or maybe it was a dog, and the room was nice and warm while the weather outside was freezing. Number Three was snuggled up and cosy. I glanced at the clock. In the old days, I'd have been just finishing up my shift at work. Heading out to get a train home. Turning up my collar to the cold and damp. Preparing to read some boring article or other to keep myself from falling asleep on the train. There was no comparison between then and now.

The next thing, someone was shaking me. The lights had gone out. Had there been a power cut? Number Three took the book off my face and I could see she was pretty grumpy with me for nodding off in the middle of the story.

"Dad, why do you fall asleep during stories? It's really annoying."

"Sorry, honey. I'm just real tired."

"You should go to bed earlier, then."

It's impossible to explain to children about the tiredness that adults feel. It's not about too little sleep, it's about too much work. Besides, if I started going to bed any earlier, I'd miss dinner.

*

It's now officially the summer because the school sports days are over. I can relax. There is no other obstacle in the way of my enjoyment. Don't get me wrong, sports days are brilliant, the kids love 'em. And the teachers work like crazy to make sure everything goes right. No, that's not the problem. It's the fathers' race that I dread.

Thankfully, neither of the sports days I attended had them. Well, okay, that's not technically true. They might have had them at the very end. But because all my children are still in the smaller classes and get to have their events first, I never hung around long enough to find out. Once the children had done their sack races, egg

and spoon races, obstacle races, relay races, three-leg-
ged races and their sprints, I was off before you could
say: "Fathers' races should be banned."

I am not speaking idly here. I am a veteran of fathers' races and I'm not yet 40. I have been that soldier,
wheezing and puffing my way across the finish line long
after the rest of the fathers have gone home for their
low-fat, high-protein teas. It is not funny. They say sport
is character building. I say, not at my age. At my age it
is destructive to the self image.

The whole of the school year you kind of swan about,
acting cool, trying to be witty, fun and intelligent, especially when another parent asks you a question that has
no big words in it. And then, after all that hard work, in
one twenty-second burst of misplaced enthusiasm, that
image you have worked so hard to create is shattered.
In that instant, they see you for what you are and no
amount of razzmatazz can change that. It is not so much
a race as a public relations disaster.

The fathers' race is the product of some sick and de-
praved imagination. I avoided the humiliation this year,
but don't think I'm getting cocky. Next year is never far
enough away. Once you go through Christmas it's a
straight run through to the summer. And once that old
cuckoo starts a-singing, I gets to thinking about those
darn fathers' races.

Speaking of which, all this stuff about hearing the
first cuckoo is a lot of tosh and piffle. People actually
write to newspapers, declaring they heard the damn bird
and could it be the first of the season? Can you believe
that? We all want to know when summer is on the way
but I mean, pleeeeaaasse!

The Government should announce a new system. It
should be the first ice cream cone, not the first cuckoo.
You can only buy an ice cream cone when the shops
start selling them again, and they only do that when the
weather gets a bit warm. My children and I bought our

first one at Teddy's of Sandycove in the County of Dublin and it had to have been the end of March. I say, could this have been a first? Jolly hockey-sticks, what?

Now, where was I? Oh, yes, children and stuff. The other night I was doing a roast chicken with potatoes, veggies and all the works. I was in the middle of making the gravy, using the juice from the chicken, and I had even started making it in the roasting dish so as not to lose any of those yummy flavours. Then, horror of horrors, I discovered I had no Bisto. So, since she-who-puts-up-with-me was home, I dashed out to the car to speed around to the shops. But no, in our house life is not that simple. The children wanted to come too. All the children. Even their pal Deirdre from next door. Which was fine except that they had no shoes on, so I had to wait. And then Number Three couldn't find her shoes at all. So I had to wait. And me with the stomach hanging out of me from hunger.

We were in the car, still waiting for Number Three, and I scratched an itch on the inside of my ear with the blunt end of a pencil. Number One saw this and next I was getting a lecture on what I can and cannot put in my ear.

"You're not supposed to put anything in your ear that's smaller than your elbow," she said sternly.

I was going to ask how you're supposed to get your elbow, or anything of a similar size, into your ear, but it wasn't the time or the place. I was too hungry. All I wanted was a packet of Bisto so I could have my dinner.

Chapter Four

When the holidays come around you can kiss goodbye your cone of silence

I've come unbelievably close to putting on my old war helmet, filling the sandbags and boarding myself up in the spare room. One or two things put me off the idea at the last minute, namely the thought that I wouldn't have any place to shave or shower and the fact that I'd never be able to take enough food with me. I may need to lose weight but I'm not that brave.

Instead I've had to accept the hard truth. The three of them are on holidays. There's no avoiding it. One way or another I have to entertain them all day every day until September.

As it is, the three of them are in super-hyper-holiday mood so I've had to be very careful. A careless slip of the tongue is enough to get them overexcited and I could end up getting badly mauled. I don't fancy having to do the ironing with one arm in a sling.

If you never knew what time of year it was, you'd work out it when holiday time had arrived because they don't need electric shock treatment to get them out of bed in the mornings. First thing now, before a single bird has sung or before the first ray of light has peeked over the horizon, they swarm out of their bedrooms looking for things to do. Fun, pre-planned, expensive kinds of things, like Bam Bams playground, or the pictures, or a visit to some relation or other who lives a two-day drive away. These children are serious play machines with no notion of what it means to lounge around the house and take things easy. They need a social secretary, not a parent.

I should have gone into serious physical training before now. Somebody out there should open a camp for
parents to go to before the schools break up for summer
so we can get in shape. Maybe the Army should run
them – that'd be more like it. Two weeks surviving in the
wilds might just be the right kind of preparation.

The thought had crossed my mind that I could make
a dash for the ferry to England and stay in hiding for the
next few months. I had to slap my face and tell myself to
cop on. I probably wouldn't have reached the front door
before being brought down by three mini rugby tackles.
That's the price you pay for being popular.

I blame the schools. It's downright irresponsible to
shut down during the summer with all that learning time
going to waste. I mean, just look at the teachers. Have
you seen a sadder lot, with their long faces, moping
around with nothing to do? They're too proud to admit
it, but I can tell they're as bored as the kids. I feel sorry
for them. The government should shake things up in
this area. Two weeks is long enough for anybody's summer holidays, I say.

But that doesn't solve the problem right now. I have
to think of ways to get the children out of the house so
they don't draw pictures on the wallpaper or start filling
the bath with moss peat and water – a mixture they love
for some reason and which they call "Elicajellica".

It's because the weather has been so yucky that a lot
of events have been taking place indoors. In-house activities which are allowed include filling the bath with
water to wash Barbie dolls; painting with water colour
paints on specified pieces of paper, while wearing over-
alls that can be dirtied; wrecking bedrooms on the
understanding that they are tidied up afterwards; any
kind of reading, music, cutting-and-pasting, doodling,
dressing up, arts and crafts; or anything which can earn
money.

In-house activities which are not allowed include

rollerblading down the stairs; cycling in the sitting room; playing drums on the piano; paint-flinging contests; wall drawing; yoghurt-smearing on furniture; fridge emptying; bare-knuckle fighting; knife throwing competitions; or anything that costs money.

The bright side to all this, in case you were wondering, is that the clock keeps ticking. One week down, eight to go.

*

Where can we go today, Dad?

I don't know about anybody else, but I'm getting asked this question every single day. If I haven't something planned, I'm in big trouble.

One day I just happened to be at the end of my tether. I'd run out of places to go and things to do. The fun cupboard was dry, unlike the weather outside at the time. So, as a kind of experiment, I told them I'd nothing planned and that we were just going to goof around the house and do very little.

The mood got pretty ugly after that. Without knowing it, I had invented a new game. I was Saddam Hussein and they were under house arrest until I decided otherwise, which might be never as far as they were concerned.

After about an hour of living in The Kingdom of Sighs, Weepings and Wailings, I gave in and took them out for a walk in their wellies and wet gear. They found the biggest puddle they could find, which was about the size of small lake, and proceeded to drench every item of clothing they had on. After that they seemed much happier in themselves.

The trick, as far as I've been able to figure out, is that they don't just need to be given something fun to do every day: they need to be given something which is different and fun to do every day. This means that going to the park only has a certain life expectancy on the

Fun-o-meter, meaning short. It also means that things which involve improving their minds, such as practising piano or going to museums or reading scientific books, are out, out, out. And don't think you can con my lot into thinking that cleaning the house is a fun and exciting game either. No way, José. These Mexican bandits which we laughingly call our children "speet" on such pathetic ideas. They want payment in gold for every job they are asked to do, preferably lodged to an offshore account. It'd be cheaper to hire the entire staff of the Shelbourne Hotel to tidy the house.

So now, although the weather is trying its best, I'm getting to the stage where I'm dreading the next rainy day. When you can't go to the beach, or get out for a walk, or play on the road or in the back garden, it really is like being in prison. All I'd have to do to complete the picture would be serve up some really bad food and call the house Alcatraz. I blame the Meteorological Service. Why can't they do something to ensure we get proper summers? If it's a case of giving them more money, then let's bend the rules on public sector pay and give it to them.

You'll find this is a common thing among parents with bored kids. Pay the money – it doesn't matter how much it is or what it's for, just pay the money so that the kids won't be bored any more. People who don't have kids do not realise what it's like being in the company of a bored Barney-lover or a numbed-out Ninja fan.

Let me put it this way, it was a well known torture during the Spanish inquisition. They'd grab a few loose women, throw them in a cell with bored kids and, before you could say Seve Ballesteros, they'd run out of the place confessing to witchcraft and begging to be burned at the stake. It was the same in World War II. Bored kids were used by British Intelligence to interrogate Jerry prisoners. Five minutes in their company and the Germans would spill the beans on the latest secret codes.

So, it's not easy trying to deal with this awesome power kids have when they're bored. Like most people, two weeks of thinking up new amusements every day has put a strain on my limited mental resources. I don't think I can hold out much longer. My only hope is if parents everywhere get together and pray for lots more sunshine. Hands together everybody, and repeat after me, "Our Father..."

*

At last, I've made it in one piece, with all body parts functioning as normal. Don't get me wrong, I love holidays when the kids are off. The lie-ins in the mornings. No lunches to make the night before. No clothes to get ready every evening.

It's keeping them amused during the day that's the hard part.

On their very first full day off the week before last, I panicked and used up all my ideas in one go. We went to McDonald's for lunch, then we went to the park where they rollerbladed 'til I was dizzy, and then we went to see *Flubber*, the movie with Robin Williams.

By the second day I was already grasping for ideas. Luckily Number One had an appointment to see the dentist, so that took up a morning. If you think that's sad, pity the poor dentist. He visited the school a week or two earlier, but what did he do? He timed his arrival for after the children's morning break. Can you imagine looking into thirty mouths after they've just eaten their snacks? Yeeeeucccchhh. Somebody send that man for retraining, quick.

No, I wasn't simply looking for ways to amuse them; I was also trying to get them used to doing little jobs around the house. She-who-has-unbroken-sleep-every-night thinks I don't get them to do enough to help. Maybe so, but it is difficult to interest them in clearing their undies out of the hot press, or putting away their own neatly ironed clothes, or clearing away the table after breakfast. The best excuse they have, and one which they employ regularly, is that they forgot I asked them to do it. The other one they have used, true as God, is: "Oh, I thought you said you *didn't* want me to clear out the hot press." I mean, what do you say?

As it is, I've just got them to the stage of pouring out their own cereals in the morning. I am now moving on to getting them to put the marmalade on their own toast. I still do the buttering. Number Two took this helpfulness a bit far the other morning. She was about to add the milk to her mini-packet of Rice Crispies when I stopped her just in time. She was putting the milk into the plastic bag with the Rice Crispies. In some areas, I have a long way to go with this family.

In the meantime, to encourage them to do little helpful jobs for me, I have had to resort to using monetary bribes. My car, which on the inside looks the way Ballyogan tip looks on the outside, is the next big project. For cleaning assistance, they will be paid handsomely. I am not at liberty to disclose the confidential remuneration package that they will receive, but I can reveal that it is more than they'd get making carpets in India and less than they'd get siphoning money out of bank accounts. One child will man (or girl) the Hoover; one will man the dustpan and brush; and one will man the Mr Sheen and duster. It shall be a sight to behold.

Which leaves me free to catch up on cultural studies, like watching the "Jerry Springer" show. It was riveting the other week. He had a series of twins on and the thing that all the different sets of twins had in common was that one of them didn't like the boyfriend or girlfriend of the other. How much does Springer pay these people? It could never be enough. You'd need lots of cash to ensure you never had to show your face in public again.

One of the sets of twins, Vanessa and Valerie, had a go at each other over Valerie's mean boyfriend. I was so embarrassed for Valerie that I had to switch the television off and go out to help with the cleaning of the car. And that's saying something.

Thankfully, the plumber called just in time and saved me from having to argue for a go of the Mr Sheen. Somebody had to keep him company while he was fixing the leak. The last thing you want is your plumber feeling lonely or left out or isolated. It is seriously hard to find one these days. Even my one will be out of action for a couple of months, so that's one less to go around. He's going to India, to see the sights – for two months. I'm enrolling on a night class in plumbing next September, just you wait and see. The flower arranging can wait.

*

There has to be a big book somewhere in which it is written that some days during the school holidays will start off great and some days will start of worse than terrible. On the good days in our house, the children rise from their beds as though lifted by the invisible hands of angels. They kind of float to the kitchen for breakfast, smiling to themselves, thinking kind thoughts. They do things like pass the sugar bowl to each other before anybody has to ask. It is like Buddha has visited the house overnight and left a meditative aura behind. We don't need words, we just nod knowingly at each other. It usually means the entire day will continue in this vein. Everything will be happiness and light. And if a cut or a scrape or a fall should threaten to bring dark clouds over our otherwise perfect day, then it will be swamped with kindness and understanding and before you know it we'll be back to happiness again.

Except, of course, there are the other days, of which there are many. These are the days when, before your foot even touches the floor for the first time in the morning, the leaves of that big imaginary book have been fluttered by the winds of Fate to open on a page where it is written "Bad Day – Watch Out". At first sight these days seem like they are going to be just like every other. There's no real time pressure to be anywhere and there might even be a nice lie-in for everybody, but slowly and surely the whole thing unravels. Alarm bells start ringing, nerves start to fray and – watch out! Bingo, you're in a bad day situation.

And so it came to pass this week. The first sign I got was when I was lying in bed recovering from a groggy dream about riding a motorcycle that wouldn't go very fast. Number Three walked in fully dressed in the same clothes she'd worn for the past two days. My request was simple: change into clean clothes. But this instruction contained a hurtful insult to the child, somehow, and sent the whole morning into a downward spiral. Next thing I heard the sound of her snuffling and crying to herself as she tore handfuls of her clothes out of the chest of drawers. She didn't like any of her clothes except the ones she was in. I wet my finger in my mouth and held it in the air. Yes, the wind was definitely changing to a cold northerly one.

Number Three's mood somehow spread to the other two because by the time we were at the breakfast table there was a low pressure front located just overhead. Breakfast was a tug-of-war between cereal boxes, the milk bottle, the toast, you name it. By the time it was over I was wondering how I was going to swing it so that I could go back to bed. Fat chance. Two of the children's friends called then to see if my lot were ready to go out to play. Before I knew it the house was full of children shouting at the tops of their voices.

Outside it was one of those rare sunny mornings. I suggested to Number Three that she wear sandals like her sisters, but that only set her off again. What was I trying to do? Turn her into a fashion victim? I let the sandals thing drop but I drew the line at allowing her to wear wellies. In the end, we compromised with runners.

Then, just when I thought it was safe to leave the kitchen, I had to withstand a barrage of abuse when I asked the three of them to line up for sun cream. This precaution gets in the way of them running straight out to play, you see. They act as though this is my favourite way of spending fifteen minutes after breakfast.

Number Two was finished first, so she ran out the door. Two seconds later a dog that nobody had ever seen before lolloped through the hall and into the sitting room. Number Three, who had had a bad morning, froze and started screaming. This set off Number One who, in turn, set the two neighbours' kids off, and created a scream-ing contest. The dog, obviously curious about all the noise, lolloped back into the hall and stopped at Number Three's frantic face, giving it an enormous lick before vanishing out the door. Nobody ever saw that dog before this epi-sode and nobody has seen it since. And it was still only nine o'clock in the morning. The phrase "pass me the jobs pages" comes to mind.

*

There's nothing like a bit of Spanish sun to take the hard-ship out of an Irish summer. The five of us went mad and went South for the past two weeks. Any country that goes to sleep in the afternoon is okay by me.

The only problem with taking a siesta, for those of us from countries where it is still an indictable crime, is trying to wake up again afterwards. The human solar panel I'm married to tried various techniques: face slap-ping, ducking my head in cold water, electrodes on my toes, that kind of thing. Oddly, the only thing that worked without fail was the promise of more wine if I kept my eyes open for thirty consecutive minutes.

The weather was mixed but when the sun came out you knew all about it. Personally I'm a Factor 20 kind of guy, but even I got a sun tan. So did the kids. And why wouldn't they? Every day we had the same routine. They played with their pals until noon, we had a swim in the pool, then we had lunch and went down to the beach for the afternoon. I followed everywhere with fifteen towels, ten swim suits, hats, goggles, beach mats, buckets, spades and emergency food and drink supplies.

Four days out of fourteen we had to get in the car and go somewhere because I needed a rest and because it was threatening to rain. On only one of those days did it actually rain. We all stepped out in it just to remember what it felt like.

When I wasn't acting as chief bag carrier, I was Florence Nightingale. In the space of the two weeks all four of them had a bout of fever at one stage or another. I lost a huge filling that had cost me £45 the week before we went away on holidays. Number One stood on a weaver fish which stung like mad for half an hour and puked in the car just the once. The breadwinner got a rash on her hands for the last few days. And Number One made the journey home with a raging sore throat and Number Two had a snuffle.

The bliss of family holidays.

So, to the best bits and the worst bits. The best bits were swimming across a narrow fish-filled estuary that was part of the beach where we stayed. I'd have preferred to have been in a very large boat armed to the teeth with spear guns, but you can't have everything. A pal we met there, a Scottish surfer called Dave, did nothing for my state of mind by shouting "Shark!" every chance he got.

Another best bit, for the adults, was the low cost of wine. I kid you not, we had a drinkable plonk for 65p which was made locally. Admittedly, I had to shave my forehead and my nose in the mornings after it, but it was great value.

Another best bit was the Spanish people who were friendly even if they didn't speak English. I made an attempt at Spanish but after telling a waiter that his mother looked like a dog's backside while trying to order food, I gave up. Another time I ordered three plates of chips for the kids and the waiter arrived with three bags of crisps on plates.

The absolutely worst bit was a visit to an Inquisition Exhibition. My idea. It was like Madame Tussaud's Horror Chamber, but without the laughs. Five minutes into this thing and Number Three was starting to gag. Ten minutes in and she had her hands permanently over her eyes. We had to leave; it was too gross. If you can imagine an exhibition that shows you a zillion slow ways to kill people, from chopping, to boiling, to hanging, then you have the gist of it. I have to take my hat off to the Spanish tourist board, they've done a marvellous job on the country since then.

The second absolutely worst bit was asking Cockney Phil next door for a taste of the Spanish black pudding he was barbecuing one night. The minute I put this stuff in my mouth I knew it was a mistake. It tasted like someone had swept the floor of a cattle ship and stuffed it into a black leather casing. The more I chewed the more he wanted to know what I thought of it. Cold beads of sweat broke out on my head.

"Lovely," I gasped as I forced it down my throat, "but a bit strong."

*

The children and their mother braved a swim in the sea this week. I knew I had done the right thing by staying on the beach when I heard the screams and squeals. The children thought it was cold, too. I have a thing about swimming in the Irish sea which is rapidly turning into a phobia. It is causing me huge problems. Should I stay on the beach eating ice cream cones, keeping a watchful eye on my offspring? Or should I just cast away my cares and jump into a radiated sea which has phosphorous bombs floating around in it? I just don't know, it's a hard one to answer.

The really hard part is whether I should pass this neurotic opinion on to my children. If I do, I could well be helping to ensure that they live longer but I am running the risk of turning them off the seaside for life. If I don't mention anything to them, they will continue enjoying the sea as normal kids do while I turn into a nervous wreck with my eyes peeled for suspicious things floating in the water.

Until I have made up my mind about the best approach, I am going to err on the side of caution and stick with the landward side of things. But don't for a minute think it is the easy option. Now that summer is upon us, this house is rapidly moving into a beach groove. Provided it's not absolutely lashing rain, my children want to be playing "Baywatch". That, of course, puts me in the role of David Hasselhoff which, I suppose, is obvious given the resemblance between us.

The hard part about going to the beach and not actually swimming is that I get landed with the role of chief architect, engineer and builder of sandcastles. Mostly the children just want a seriously large hole dug in the sand. That's fair enough. I have no problem with repetitive, manual labour which involves very little thought. After all, am I not a man?

The children, for their part, seem to instinctively know when it's deep enough to suit their requirements. They take one look at my perspiration-soaked T-shirt, observe my short, gasping breaths and judge, that's it, the hole is ready. Then they jump in and out of it for about three hours while I lie down and recuperate like some beached whale.

Recently, though, things have taken a turn for the worse. The good old reliable deep hole is no longer enough to satisfy their sophisticated tastes. Now the children want magic fairy castles or Aztec cities or, don't laugh because this was a serious request, sports cars made out of sand. I have made these things. My aching back is testament to my sandy endeavours. I don't mind; it's a small price to pay if it means I get to keep my toes dry and other bits of me at the body temperature God intended.

Speaking of God, I happened to be down Arklow way recently and couldn't help noticing a sign in the car park of one of the big churches in the town. It said: "Beware. Birds Dropping Dangerous Objects." It seems that Arklow birds have a fondness for picking up heavy objects and flying over people's heads and then dropping these things on them. Will somebody please phone David Attenborough?

But when you think about it, a whole range of possibilities opens up, doesn't it? That neighbour you don't like? Get a seagull to drop an anvil on his head. The bank manager who wouldn't give you an overdraft? Train a crow to drop a horseshoe on him, preferably with the horse still attached.

Another strange thing I noticed this week is that when the weather gets any way good, people who go out to work begin to hate me. All winter long I'd got tons of sympathy, especially if it was raining and cold. Workers would be looking at me, thinking: "Poor sod, out driving kids around while we're cosy at work." Then, as soon as the sun began to shine, it changed to: "What are you so happy about, you smug bugger?" In future I'm not going to mention how often we go to the beach because some people obviously can't take it.

*

I'm determined my children will receive the best possible education for life that they can get. That's why I insisted the other afternoon that they all sit down with me and watch *Spartacus*, starring Kirk Douglas and Laurence Olivier. Normally I wouldn't, but when a classic movie like this comes along you have to make exceptions. And besides, we're on holidays.

I know the sun was shining outside and they should have been out playing in it, getting fresh, healthy air into their lungs. However, sometimes there are important things to be done and you just have to stay in and do them. Like watching *Spartacus*.

There's one particular scene where a snooty Olivier says to Tony Curtis, who's been captured by the Romans: "You'll be my body slave."

Number One was fascinated by this. She asked me what a body slave was. I have to admit that I didn't have a clue but I made up a fairly convincing answer – later shown to be correct – about how a body slave washes you in the bath, dresses you and dries your hair. Then it dawned on me.

"It's exactly what I do for you," I said excitedly, fascinated by my own discovery. "I'm your body slave."

"Oh, right," she said, completely underwhelmed.

"No, really, I wash you and I dress you, sometimes, and I dry your hair and..."

"Dad, do you mind," she said, "I'm trying to watch *Spartacus*."

"Sorry."

"And could you turn it up a bit?"

"Certainly, love."

The following day the sun still happened to be shining. In fact, I look back on those two days and I think it was probably the best summer we've had in years. It was a Saturday and I was away visiting, so my wife took the children to the beach, along with Number Three's boyfriend. The two tots were playing this game of making a picnic out of sand and then handing it to she-who-must-be-encouraged-to-seek-regular-pay-rises.

Number Three would hand over the sand and say: "Here, servant, take this." Eventually, the boyfriend said to her, "Why do you need a servant when you have parents?"

Isn't it uncanny? Isn't it amazing how that idea, of having parents as slaves, takes root in such young minds? Why do you need a servant when you have parents? I find myself asking the very same question. Why, indeed? I'm just short of wearing a frilly apron and hat, and bowing to them every time they ask for something.

My main concern, though, is that if I'm a cooking, bathing, dressing, chauffeur service now, what happens when they get older? If it goes on like this I'm probably going to have to find real boyfriends for them when they're teenagers and sit the Leaving Cert for them and all. I may even get a job for them when their schooling is done and then hand over the wage packet at the end of every week.

I really hope it doesn't go that far because I'm kind of looking forward to having my own life when they're older. I find myself looking enviously at old people who play bowls all day long, wishing I could be in there behind the railings playing with them. Or are they doing it for their children who are at home watching Kirk Douglas in *Spartacus*?

I keep telling myself, relax, everything will be okay, they'll grow up and form a mega-successful girl band and I can retire to Italy and drink white wine all day long. You've no idea how that thought cheers me up.

Speaking of being cheered up, here's my Quote of the Week.

Number One looks up at the steeple of the local church, which has a cross on top that looks exactly like a Christmas decoration, and says: "That's a bit early, isn't it, Dad?"

*

We have just returned from a two-week holiday in County Clare. I'm not saying the weather was bad because some days were lovely. But when you've unpacked an entire car load of beach thingies and stripped down to your manly togs only to have the heavens open on you, it's too much.

The way we did it was we kept the heating in the cottage on to dry out clothes and towels. When the rain got really bad we had piggyback races through the rooms of the cottage. We were staying in a lovely spot north of Kilkee and thankfully there was a festival there for our first week.

The girls entered a fancy dress competition, the two youngest as princesses and the oldest as a farmer. The princesses won a trophy and the farmer won a medal. There were eleven entrants altogether, which included two Father Teds and Mrs Doyles; one Ben Dunne covered in pound notes; one clown; two Action Men; and a group of nurses called "The Cutbacks" with a teddy on a stretcher; plus one walking wounded who looked like he needed the attention of The Cutbacks.

After the prize-giving the girls were allowed to march in the parade up and down the main street. One of the floats in the parade featured Ben Dunne, Charles Haughey and Margaret Heffernan playing cards on the back of a tractor trailer. Lying beside them with a white face was a dead body with a sign reading: "Des Traynor, RIP."

Another night we bundled down to watch a duck race in the river. I couldn't for the life of me figure out how they trained ducks to race, which is why I wanted to go. It turned out they threw plastic bottles with numbers on them into the river and these were the "ducks". Did I feel stupid? There was a wheelbarrow race planned for the following night, but I told she-who-is-up-at-the-crack-of-dawn that there was no way I was going because there probably wouldn't be any real wheelbarrows in it.

Every night I took the family sea fishing at various places. I caught absolutely nothing. In an attempt to involve the children I'd let Number One hold the weight while I put bait on the hooks – until one night she hooked me in the thumb. When I stopped dancing "The Walls of Limerick" I asked her how she managed to do that.

"I was just holding the weight and throwing it from one hand to the other hand and it dropped," she said.

We met up with friends for a few days. One of their daughters had a virtual dog, those little computer gizmo whatsits that you have to walk and feed and all that. Hers died. We watched it go to heaven on little computer wings. I was inconsolable.

Speaking of inconsolable, my lawyers have instituted proceedings against the National Lottery. When I'm in Dublin, somebody in the West wins the jackpot. When I'm in the West, somebody in Dublin wins the jackpot. This is more than coincidence. This is a campaign against me personally. They have been asked to cease and desist from this practise forthwith or else face the full rigour of the law.

We went to Kilkee's "waterworld" too. I forgot my togs so I had to buy a pair. A 36 waist, please, I said to the "Baywatch" girl behind the counter. Off I go, only to return. A 38 waist, please, I said, blushing slightly. Then once more. A 40 waist, please, I said with a bag over my head. But they had none. Imagine King Kong squeezed into Cheetah the Chimp's togs and you'll get the picture.

I had so much fun in waterworld that I couldn't remember the PIN number for my cash card afterwards. The whole family was sitting in The Pantry on the main street, eating all around them, and I couldn't get any money out. I went back to join them, in a sweat. When I stopped crying and broke it to she-who-makes-no-mistakes-like-this that I faced a life of servitude in that cafe, Number One overheard and was able to trot out the number with ease. The child was showered with gifts in abundance and we all lived happily ever after. Even the sun came out that day.

*

The "knicker trick" has been banned. It has served the children well all summer but now, like all good things, it has had to end. She-who-eats-'til-she's-full-not-'til-she's-tired has decreed it so. To tell you the truth I hadn't noticed the knicker trick being particularly harmful. It must be one of those male-female things.

Every time we went to the beach, the children out of modesty would put their swim togs on over their knickers. Then we'd go through a five minute wriggling competition as each of them tried to stretch one leg of their knickers far enough to get one leg out. Once that awkward but masterly accomplishment had been achieved, the knickers could be taken off with almost stylish ease. This was what became known in our house as the "knicker trick".

Last weekend was its grand finale. It was a scorcher and it will probably be one of the last beach trips we'll do this year. Two days earlier, while sorting out a mountain of laundry with me, the-woman-whose-true-identity-is-Hawkeye noticed that three – no – four pairs of knickers had been destroyed by this contortionist routine. From that moment on, the knicker trick's days were numbered. And so it came to pass. It will not appear at swimming pools throughout the winter. Instead, it must slip into the memory and folklore of our family and this painfully brief note must be its last lament.

Speaking of lament, am I sorry that years ago I stopped jogging and running and generally doing exercises that involve the use of my legs? Absolutely. Why? Because we had a parents' relay race with a gang of people some weeks ago and nothing would do the children but that I'd enter it. No amount of special pleading or the furnishing of doctor's certificates would pacify them. I had to run in it or else they weren't going to talk to me ever again.

I have to admit I thought about this latter possibility for quite a while. But it was no use. It would be too confusing at meal times and other points of contact during the day if they decided not to speak to me. It's confusing enough as it is.

So off I went, first to run in my team, in a race that had three teams. Were we mad? Most probably. Remember, there was no training for this. I just went out there, like everybody else, and ran. All the children, mine included, were lined up waiting to see how their Dads and Mums would do. The starter said "Go!" and, when I went, all I can remember thinking is: "Are my legs working?" It felt like I had nothing from the knees down. I must have looked like Toulouse Lautrec, the French painter with the height problem, or Groucho Marx in a hurry.

I tore off down the track and had to run around another person and then run back. My children were shouting "Dad, Dad, Dad!" and I was thinking, "Mad, Mad, Mad!" In the end our team won and the three degrees were suitably impressed with my sorry attempt at running. Isn't that what's great about being a parent? Your kids think well of you all the time, even when you're dying on your feet.

Speaking of dying, I had the full complement plus a pal out last Monday to buy new shoes for Number Three before she started big school. When you have to go out with one of them, you have to go out with all of them. Is it clever to buy shoes the day before school reopens? It would be, if half the country didn't insist on doing it at the same time. Getting the shoes was not the problem. The problem was the age-old one of being in a very busy town with a gang of kids, miles from the car and only halfway through the shopping list, when Number Three told me she wanted to do a pee.

It took a ten-minute walk before we could find a toilet, down a crowded street, across a busy road, into a shopping centre and up to the top floor. If the Government is serious about the Constitution, which states that the family is the basic unit of society, then it really should get its act together. There should be toilets everywhere so that kids who are taken short can do a pee. In fact, there should an amendment to the Constitution which states that "wheresoever the said unit of society might find itself taken short, the citizens constituting that unit should have an inviolable right to a clean toilet not less than twenty yards from their said persons".

*

I'm treating the Easter school holidays as a mini version of the summer holidays. I've got through the first week but the bad news is that I'm exhausted already. The good news should have been that we can all sleep late into the mornings, but a lie-in for my lot ends at a quarter past seven.

What kills me is that during school term I have to use a forklift to get them out of bed, but in holiday time they wake just before the first light has crept over the horizon and they lie there, waiting to jump out of bed and start chasing and screaming their heads off.

The youngest one has a routine. She comes in and turns the bed into downtown Beirut in twenty-two seconds flat. Then she asks if she can go and watch TV. I mumble that she can, knowing that I'll get at least another twenty seconds before she's bored and comes back looking for brekky.

I've tried having something for them to do every day. They're still too young to do carpentry or paint any rooms, so it's had to be a kiddy-friendly menu.

The other day we went to the park. I left the car on

double yellow lines close to the gate, but the children wouldn't get out of the car because they said we'd go to jail for illegal parking. I had to drive around until I found a space they all agreed was legitimate and safe. So, after a twenty-minute walk, in we went. First I pushed Number Three on the swings and then ran to watch Number Two coming down the fireman's pole. Then Number One wanted a hand crossing the monkey bars. At the end of that, Number Three's swing was slowing down. Imagine this routine for about an hour and you'll get a flavour of what a trip to the park involves.

To finish off, we went to play on the bandstand; Number Two fell off and scraped her leg. I got tired of the park all of sudden and threw them back in the car and went home.

Another day I took them to the cake shop for a morning treat. I sat down to drink my mug of coffee, extra strong, and noticed their cakes and milk were finished already. "Will you be long, Dad?" they asked, itching to get on to the next exciting adventure.

Then there was the trip to the local pool. The water was roasting and the lifeguard had to help me out because I was getting lightly broiled. I lay down on the bench in the dressing rooms while the kidlets pretended they were Apache Indians and did naked war dances.

I won't go into the trip to the Powerscourt Waterfall, other than to say the place is well named because all the children did was fall in water. They tell me they had a ball but I found the experience a bit like "Baywatch on Rocks". My back was in a serious state from lugging bodies out of water which was, of course, a millimetre deeper than the average kiddie wellie.

Old people tell me it'll all be worth it in the end. Personally, I think I must have been really bad in a former life.

*

If Mel Brooks ever decides to make a movie about me, I've got the title for him: *Raising Saddles*. All last weekend with the good weather I was like a glorified bicycle mechanic. The saddle on one was too low, on the other too high, and on the third it kept swivelling about like a spinning top. I went around permanently with one of those multi-headed bike spanners in my pocket, just waiting for the next breakdown.

Before they could even ride out into the sunshine, all the tyres needed pumping because they hadn't been used since the last good weather. The gears on Number One's bike kept slipping and then a mudguard had to be taken off. And don't get me started about Number Three's helmet.

Day in, day out, I tell her she must wear her helmet when she's on her bike. Okay, I admit she has stabilisers on the bike so there is only a small likelihood of her having a tumble. Still, a parent can never be too careful.

So there I was over the weekend, telling her repeatedly: "Put your helmet on before you get on that bike." Eventually, by Bank Holiday Monday, the sun was so hot and she was so fed up with me that I heard her running up the road, helmet in hand.

"Everything all right?" I enquired.

"Take this," she said, firing the helmet at me. Luckily I ducked because it banged off the wall behind me.

"You're supposed to wear that," I shouted after her as she made a dash for it.

"It's too hot," she shouted back without even stopping.

"You must wear it," I said, raising my voice as she got further and further away.

"No way," she shouted back just before she disappeared around the corner.

I don't know. Maybe I'm doing something wrong here. In the old days kids used to do what they were told. Or maybe it's just the words I use.

Call me nuts, but I can't find the right words in English sometimes to describe the simplest of things. I asked Number Two to turn on the immersion for the baths the other night while I was trying to cook one of those complicated dinners which have meat and two veg. All I needed to say was: "Make sure both switches are down." What did I do instead? I started off with a long rigmarole about where the hot press was and where the switches were on the wall inside the door and all about the switch on the left and the switch on the right.

"Which is left, Dad? This hand?"

"Yeah, that hand. There's another switch beside it on the right."

"Which is the right, Dad? This hand?"

"Yeah, that's your right. Anyway, the switch on right is probably up so I want you to switch that down."

"Switch it down."

"Right."

"On the left?"

"No, on the right."

"Right."

Off she went and then a few minutes later she shouted back to me that both switches were up, which wasn't in the plan. Then I got confused and I couldn't remember if up was on or off.

"Does it say 'On' or 'Off'?" I shouted as I drained the steaming hot potatoes.

"I don't know," came the reply.

"Okay, the switch on the left – does it say 'Sink' or 'Bath'?" I shouted again, noticing the black smoke coming from the grill pan.

"Which is the left again?"

All I could do was tell her to leave it; I'd fix it when I'd cooked the dinner. In fact, I was so tired out by then that I didn't bath them at all. Some nights I just don't have the energy.

The following night was a much better night for it

anyway because Number One had been playing with slime all day and she needed a bath big time. You can buy slime for kids, you know. My one saved up for a Slime File, which is a kind of Filofax for gross kids. You get a free packet of green slime, which is like a Day-Glo playdough-from-hell. The folder itself is full of horrible concoctions to make and horrible stickers of snotty noses and cut-off fingers. It's also got jokes:

"What's green and smells? Answer: A frog's bum!"

Charming, don't you think? My sentimental fatherly notion that these girls are going to grow up to be princesses is fast disappearing.

Chapter Five

Is that a migraine coming on – or is the season of peace and goodwill just around the corner?

"'Tis the season to be jolly, tra-la-la-la-la, la-la-la-la!"

I love the smell of puddings boiling on the cooker, don't you? I love the sound of laughter and gaiety, of jolliness, joyfulness and all those other J-words. But hark, before we get to the season of peace and goodwill, we have to go through the season of stress, anxiety and migraines.

When I say stress, anxiety and migraines, I don't just mean shopping for presents. A trip to Clery's in the rain, with five of us, four umbrellas and one buggy, is only part of it. Down in the bags section in the basement, two suddenly need to do a pee, and the nearest toilet on the first floor. All the escalators that go up are further away than the escalators coming down. The queue for the ladies is a mile long. We're all wearing coats and it's roasting. And two of the princesses are moaning about having to use the men's instead.

No, that's too narrow. I had something broader in mind.

I boiled the pud last week. I used the pressure cooker. I know why they call them pressure cookers now. It's because when you use one of them there is serious pressure on you to make sure that you're using it properly. How was I to know that the rubber seal thingy was old and needed replacing?

It should have been a perfectly cooked bowl of steamed plum pudding. Instead, what emerged from the cooker would have fetched $2m in an Andy Warhol exhibition. Plastic bowls do not look pretty when they melt; they do not smell attractive, either. And pressure cookers are dang hard to clean when they've nuked the food.

In a panic, I rang she-who-must-not-be-pulled-out-of-meetings-to-solve-little-domestic-crises. She was in a meeting, but this was an emergency. I poured my heart out as I was pouring the pressure cooker contents into the bin. She understood. It was cool, it was okay, everything would be fine. It could happen to anybody. Why, she was sure there were people with all of their brains intact who could have made that kind of mistake.

The next day Number One had her first piano exam, Number Two went into hospital to have a birthmark removed from her arm, Number Three stayed at home with chicken pox, the chimney sweep came to sweep the chimney, the Telecom man came 'cos the phone sounded like all our friends had moved to Estonia, and the gas men were coming to change me over to the brave new world of natural gas.

Number One did the piano exam and I sat outside the door on the edge of my seat, a nervous wreck. I knew all the tunes by heart. I could hear her playing "Twinkle, Twinkle Little Star" when she paused the teensiest bit too long. Myself and a teenage girl who was waiting her turn held our breath until we could hear the music play again. I looked at the teenager's music book and it was the same as Number One's: she knew the pieces off by heart too.

Number Two did fine in hospital but came home a bit groggy from the anaesthetic and lay on the couch all that afternoon. Mr O'Neill came and swept the chimney and told us he was retiring because his sons had got jobs in Telecom. The Telecom man came but he didn't seem to know anything about this. Thankfully, he knew something about phones, fixed my problem and left, not long after Mr O'Neill. Then the gas company men came, but within three minutes were able to tell me that I couldn't have natural gas because of the layout of the boiler room. I signed up for natural gas last August in the mistaken belief it would take three weeks. I waited three months, got surveyed by a gas engineer, had five holes dug in the ground around my house, had a meter box fitted outside, and at the last minute they tell me something I could have been told last summer? Was I a teensy bit irate? Answers on a teddy bear, please.

So, let's recap on the two things we've learned today. Pressure cookers are so named because using one puts you under serious pressure and the gas company is so named because it's a gas company.

*

Things are gearing up for Christmas, big time. Number Three is going around with her Fisher Price ghetto blaster, playing Christmas carols at top volume. "Away in a Manger" and "Hark the Herald Angels" are swimming in my head. To add to the atmosphere, she sings along at the top of her voice, doing her best imitation of an angel in the heavenly choir. I haven't the heart to tell her she's giving me a serious headache. In fact, her singing is so bad that the other two dug out a Fisher Price walkman that one of the cousins left behind and placed it strategically on her bed. They know that if they tell her out straight to use it instead of the ghetto blaster she'll do the opposite. Clever kids, those. We are all waiting in the hope that she takes the bait.

Underpinning the Christmas theme, the same child came home from school the other day and told me her trousers were dirty.

"Why are they dirty?" I asked.

"I was on the floor in the classroom," she said.

"Why were you on the floor in the classroom?"

"Because I'm a lamb."

"A what?"

"A lamb."

"Why?"

"Because we're doing that song, you know the one that goes rum-pa-pom-pom."

"Oh, right."

"And some people are cows but I'm a lamb."

The three of them are getting closer to deciding what they want from Santa. Nothing's been decided yet, you understand, but the huddles have been forming and the discussions have been taking place. The important thing is not only to ask for something they really want, but also something the other two think is pretty cool.

Number One is growing up now, though, and if I can use code here for a minute, things might be different in her own mind about certain things this year. I'm not sure and I can't swear to it. It's just a hunch. A measure of how grown up she's getting was when I rushed to answer the phone the other day and it was for her. One of her friends needed to check something they'd got for homework.

It's such a big occasion when the phone rings in our house. I thought it might have been the Lottery ringing me up to admit a foul blunder last week or 98FM with a £1,000 cash call. But, no. Barely concealing my bitter disappointment, I called Number One and told her it was for her. She breezed by the kitchen door and said: "I'll take it in the sitting room." In the sitting room, no less! Well, pardon me, Mrs Hoity-toity! I'll just hang on here until you're ready to take your phone call! I imagined my dear departed mother looking down on this from Heaven going: "Yeeesssss!"

The other time I did a double take during the week was when Number Three came home for lunch. She was only in the door, had dumped her school bag in the middle of the hall, flicked off her shoes in all directions, left her coat on the stairs and headed straight for the television. Over her shoulder she muttered, "Any post for me?" This kid is only five years of age! Who is going to be sending her letters? Is there something going on here that I don't know about?

Number Two had her moment as well this week and it had me rolling around holding my head for the laughter, because I knocked my neck out of joint, so it was painful to laugh, if you follow me. Anyway, she was at the tea table looking pretty glum, so I asked her what was wrong.

"Nothing," she said, which is always a clue that something is wrong.

"Come on, tell me. What's worrying you?"

"Well," she said reluctantly, "it's Brownies."

I was surprised to hear this because she's been loving Brownies. She has her uniform, her sash, has got two badges, knows how to wear her woggle, how to give the Brownie sign, and knows the Brownie promise inside out. So what could it have been?

"Has someone been nasty to you?" I enquired.

"No," she said.

"Tell me. What is it?"

"It's just that next week we have to be unrolled."

"Unrolled?"

"Yeah, and I'm a bit scared of it."

"No, love, I think they mean *en*rolled."

"What's enrolled?"

"They just take your name down and put it on the roll with all the other names, like in school."

"Oh."

May problems always be as easy to resolve as this one.

*

I have a bone to pick with Coca Cola. Why did they have to run their "polar bears pushing home the Christmas tree" ad so early? November 3, it was. I remember because I checked the date when I saw it on the telly. Don't they realise what happens when they do that? The children start thinking about you-know-who. For God's sake, they've only just packed away their Hallowe'en costumes.

As if Coke hasn't got enough money, it has to start hyping us up for the Festive Season already. By my calculations, and it was a tough one because sums were never my strongest subject, they triggered my children into thinking about Christmas all of fifty-one days in advance. Now, I ask you, is this right? And it wasn't just Coke. I heard one shopping centre advertising on the radio with a Christmas theme even earlier than that.

If triggers like this lead them, on average, to mention what they'd like to get for Christmas just twice a day, then that's three twos by 365 over 52 divided by 12 and the square root of... which is, um, a heck of a lot of times for me to listen to it. That's why I've come up with a solution.

There should be a special committee set up by Government to oversee this whole thing. The Christmas season should not be allowed to start until two to three weeks, at the very maximum, before the day itself. Anyone found dressing a shop window or advertising with a Christmas theme before this start date should be taken out and flogged and then made to pay a hefty fine. The opposite would also be the case. Anyone who holds off hyping Christmas should get a tax break, so that the longer he or she holds off, the bigger the tax break.

This is what Americans call a win-win situation. Any politician proposing it would get the votes of all the parents in the country. The Church would be happy because it is would be taking commercialism out of what is essentially a spiritual festival. The only people who are going to hate it are big businesses, but that's only because they haven't thought it out properly. What the money merchants forget is that, no matter what, all us little people are still going to have to buy exactly the same amount of stuff. Also, they get to save a bundle on not having to advertise so early. It makes perfect sense to me, but then I'm just a househusband. What would I know?

Something I do know is that we have a wasps' nest in the house. It's in the sitting room, but I don't know whether it's in the ceiling or under the floor. For the past five weeks I've been living every horror movie director's dream. The room is a scene of carnage, bloodshed and mayhem, as I whack, squish and spray my way through my daily quota of wasps.

I've searched everywhere but I can't find the nest. I even tried befriending individual wasps in the hope that they might lead me back to their home. No luck. For ages I kept telling myself that they had to be coming in from the outside. These are the lies you tell yourself when you are in denial. It was an easy one to believe, too. Remember, I have children who have not yet figured out that the hall door must be encouraged to close by humans; it simply will not it do it on its own.

She-who-will-make-the-plum-puddings-this-year gave me a funny look when I mentioned this theory. Okay, it probably did sound a bit daft. Every day a dozen or so drowsy, drunken wasps would have to hide outside the door, not letting a careless buzz or giggle escape their lips, and then, as soon as I opened the hall door, slip in quietly one by one to my sitting room.

In the end I rang a wasp exterminator. A woman with a voice like Arnold Schwarzenegger told me it would cost £50 for them to come out "und deal vit ze nest of vaspies". Also, because I didn't know where the nest was, it meant that the meter would be running until they found it. But then, and this is what I like about this lil' ol' country, she gave me a break. She told me to save my £50 because the wasps are dying off and they never return to the same nest. So, if I wait it out, they'll be gone in a matter of days. It was a nice thing for her to do. It felt like Christmas had come early.

*

The letters to Santa are being written. When they're finished, though, I'm not to post them. The children need time to mull over the choices they've made. They have to be sure that what they've asked for is really, *really* what they want.

Number Two knew exactly what she wanted and wrote out her letter in flash: a Polly Pocket Beauty and the Beast and a thing called Squand which only she has seen advertised on the telly. She also asked Santa if Rudolph and Mrs Claus were keeping well.

Number One is still only halfway through her letter because she's humming and hawing over a few options, none of which she has revealed to me or her mother. The few hints dropped all refer to expensive, high-tech gadgetry. We're waiting with bated breath to see if Santa Claus is going to be tested to the limits of endurance this year.

Until last week Number Three had a major crush on a Barbie scooter, but now it isn't even on the subs bench for some reason. She wants three things instead: first, a watch; secondly, a Boyzone CD, which I'm glad Santa is sending so I don't have to go into a shop and actually buy it; and, thirdly, she wants a... a... a...

We had a small problem for a while over Number Three's third choice. She couldn't figure out what she wanted. She was broken-hearted when she found out that the elves don't make Batgirl suits, but only Batman suits. She has a Batman suit already. I agreed with her that it was unfair to girls and sympathised; maybe next year Santa might get around to making them.

Number Two's attempt at a helpful solution, that she might ask Santa to send Number Three a photo of

Rudolph, was not appreciated by her younger sister, so Number Two didn't offer any more suggestions. In desperation we got out the Toymaster catalogue and she had a browse. Fortunately her eyes fell upon the very thing she wanted. Santa has now been asked to bring her Buckaroo!

I also took the three of them in to see Santa in Arnotts department store. I was in the queue about ten minutes and we hadn't moved a centimetre when I realised Santa was on his lunch break. Thirty minutes later it was our turn to enter his magical cavern, complete with polar bears, Eskimos, and penguins flapping their wings. It was £3 in, which included a photo with Santa. Three young ones with a baby came out as we were going in and one of them said: "Ah, Jaysz, that was scabby."

"What's scabby mean, Dad?" asked Number Three.

"I don't know, love," I lied.

In we went and the three of them were so gobsmacked, because he really did look the part, that they couldn't answer any of his questions. Eventually Santa had to ask me to get off his knee so that he could talk to the kids a bit better. And still they weren't telling him what they were going to ask for Christmas. I was left answering all the questions, like Santa's little interpreter. Then they had their picture taken with him and we left. It was all over in a flash, if you'll pardon the pun, and they came out wishing they'd got a small present. I'm sure the photos will be lovely when I saddle up the horse and ride back in to town to collect the darn things, but I think Arnotts should give parents the option for their £3 of either a photo or a pressie. I think pressies would win that contest easily.

The Advent calendars have been opened too. She-who-can-leap-small-buildings-with-a-single-bound bought two of them, one for the kitchen and one for the children's bedrooms. The over-generous act of a compensating working parent? Perhaps, but it caused no end of discussion. Who would open the first calendar window on the first day? And who would open the second calendar window on the first day? And what about the person who didn't get to open either of them on the first day? And wasn't it unfair on the child who didn't get to open one first? After I'd pulled out what remained of my hair, I decided to leave them at it and, lo, they came to a dandy solution. Number Two opened the kitchen one first. Number Three opened the bedroom one first. And Number One gets to open both of them on the last day, which is Christmas Eve, no matter whose turn it is on that day. Peace and goodwill is shining all around.

*

For most people, the twelve days to Christmas start today. At our house they started in November. The kids have all bought each other presents. And mine, I hope. The cakes and puds are made. The Christmas cards are already written and are just about to be sent. The two Advent calendars are going at full throttle. Regarding same calendars, we had to install a complicated and sophisticated roster system so that I would never, ever, ever have to hear those nerve rattling words again: "Whose turn is it today, Dad?"

Now everything is as it should be in the Universe. Except, of all the blessed things to get hit with at this time of year, I'm beginning to get maudlin. It's a fact. I'm enjoying the build-up to the season of goodwill so much that I'm starting to get worried about missing it when it's gone. Can you believe that? I keep asking myself, what'll it be like when they're grown up? For one thing, Christmas won't last half as long. It'll probably start on Christmas Eve and end on St Stephen's Day.

As it is, I've had three weeks of a build-up already and I still have the excitement of buying and decorating the Christmas tree, the school's carol service, the Brownies carol service, the holly wreath for the door, the house decorations, bringing home the turkey, the presents under the Christmas tree, the excitement on Christmas morning, the turkey and pud dinner, and the blockbuster movie on TV.

I keep wishing there was a drug you could give children which would keep them this age for ever. No, on second thought, scrap that idea. I wouldn't have the energy to keep going at this pace for the rest of my life. God probably invented old age so that parents would get a rest from their kids.

Still, I get a bit like an old granny at this time of year. Tears well up when the children start talking about hanging up their stockings. Normally they wouldn't hang up anything in a fit, but Christmas is different, isn't it? It brings out the angel in them and the eejit in us.

I've a sneaking suspicion this is all coming to a head because I met a woman the other night whose children are grown up and she told me to enjoy mine while I could. She was getting maudlin too. We were just short of having a good cry together. I told her I thought that was good advice except for one teensy thing. I'm too busy parenting, too busy dealing with them, too busy cooking and minding and ferrying and refereeing on disputes to appreciate them.

"Yeah," she said, taking the hanky I offered her, "it was like that for me as well."

Maybe I need an *au pair*, or a full-time minder. Then I could sit back and make it my full-time occupation to appreciate my kids. I could enjoy their little squabbles knowing I didn't have to intervene and find out who poked who in the eye first and whether it was on purpose. I could enjoy their scatty personalities as they struggle into mismatched clothes with only ten minutes to go before school starts. I could learn to love the way they instantly drop something on the floor the absolute moment that object ceases to interest them.

Yes, from a distance I could really learn to appreciate them. But, first, I don't want another minder living in the house. Been there, done that, didn't like it. Secondly, I can't afford one. Even if I could, I know I'd start taking on extra work and before you know it, I'd be out of the house as often as I was when I worked full time. Every time I've had an offer of one sort or another I've had to go through this same mental exercise and eventually I end up at the same conclusion. I did not give up my job to go back to work. That's why I've turned down loads of offers because they were going to involve me being out of the house, or else being in the house but locked away working every hour I could. It was nice to be asked, though.

No, I think I'll continue on my own merry way. Immersed in children would be the proper phrase for it. Up to my neck in them. Knee deep in them. Flooded with them. Out the door with them. Saturated. Swamped. But with them.

*

Seat belts on, we are now entering hyper-hysteria mode. This is a notch higher up the scale from the plain old hysteria mode in which the children have been living for the past two weeks. The Big Day is just around the corner. It's so close they can almost reach out and touch it.

The waiting is driving them into such a tizzy that I am having difficulty understanding them when they speak. And, when it's my turn to speak to them, I have to make sure they are watching my lips very closely. Then they must nod to let me know they have understood.

To try and take their minds off things in the final run-up, I have been creating all sorts of diversions. I dug out the Christmas stockings a little early on purpose. Even they thought it was early but I told them there's no use in all of us running around on Christmas Eve wondering

where we put them last year. The stockings are too important to leave to the last minute. We took them to the
fireplace and marked out the exact spot where each of
their stockings will hang. If one claims another's place
on that mantelpiece, someone will die. I just have that
feeling about it.

We've also had a family powwow about what exactly
we are leaving out for Santa on Thursday night. In a
unanimous decision, the Murphy jury has voted for two
mince pies and a glass of milk for the Big Guy and a
carrot, peeled but not chopped, for Rudolph.

Oh, of course, the tree is now up. We decorated it
while Number Three's tape of Christmas carols played at
warp factor nine in the background. They all sang along,
the fire was lit, and all we needed was Bing Crosby building a snowman in the garden to complete the picture.

Meanwhile, there I was trying to cope with fifteen
feet of Christmas tree that wouldn't stand on its own
three legs. We have a very precious angel which goes on
top every year. My big fear is always that it'll fall off,
smash into pieces and that this will be an omen for the
start of a disastrous, cursed Christmas. I'm supersti-
tious like that. That's why this angel only gets taken out
of its box at the very last minute. Normally, I get on the
ladder only after the children have all been positioned
around me holding out a blanket in case I have to jump.

As for getting them out of the house, she-who-is-
downright-perfect-in-every-way has everything so
organised I have to invent reasons to go downtown. I
make excuses like visiting the butcher to make sure he
has our order for the turkey. Yes, he will say patiently,
he has our order. He's had it for two weeks. It's for one,
big mother of a turkey for the family who visits him every
two days to ask how the turkey is coming on. He is a
patient, patient man. I like him. Mainly because he hasn't
told me to go away.

Then we go to the supermarket to do some shopping. If you go into a supermarket with three children at Christmas time you are asking for trouble. Yet this is exactly what you have to do. What other choice is there? Tie them to a lamp-post outside? Don't answer that.

Halfway through one particular Christmas shopping trip from hell this week I was thinking about going to the DIY shop and buying a thick rope. Numbers Two and Three had a great time playing chasing up and down the aisles. Nobody else seemed to be enjoying it quite as much as they were, for some reason.

I've even been going to the dry cleaner's more than I need to. I lost one of the tickets this week and when I went back and explained to the man behind the counter that the ticket had been for a black lady's suit, he said: "A black lady's suit, eh? Changed wives, have you?"

I laughed at that one, on the inside. Everyone's a comedian at Christmas for reasons I've never fully understood. I don't think I can take much more of it. Please Santa, hurry up and come. I've been a good boy all year, honestly, but I'd like a rest now, if you wouldn't mind.

*

Santa came. Isn't he a marvel? At six in the morning on the Big Day, I felt a hot little nose press up against mine. I opened my bleary eyes and there was this huge pair of excited brown eyes looking at me. I thought, "Did somebody buy a St Bernard without telling me?" Then I remembered what day it was. I groaned and tried to pull the covers over my head on the remote chance that I'd be left alone. No way, José! I got dragged out of bed to see what Santa had left. Overlooking the fact that he and Rudolph had left a mess of crumbs from the carrot and the mince pies, which I pointed out grumpily to she-who-was-elected-to-make-breakfast, he was extremely good to the children. Through half-closed eyes I got to play with a Game Boy, dress Number Three up as Batman, and even have Baby Born pee on my knee. And this was all before breakfast. I felt obliged to point out to Number Two that Baby Born not only pees and poohs, but she can also puke. Naturally, she wanted to see how this happened but I hadn't the stomach to show her at that hour of the morning. Nothing dampens enthusiasm for playtime better than having had only two hours of sleep.

At least Santa didn't leave soot all over the carpet, the way he did in a friend's house one year. Another pal remembers his children going downstairs one year to find a ghastly smell in the sitting room. What had naughty Rudolph left behind him on the carpet? You guessed it: a big pile of reindeer droppings, which looked incredibly like horse pooh. So I suppose a few crumbs is nothing in comparison.

I have always believed the children must be encouraged away from presents that take a lot of assembly on Christmas day. I don't know how Meccano sells a single box. And as for Airfix! Anybody giving or bringing an Airfix model into our house on Christmas day is guaranteed a bowl of plum pudding over his head.

I am on a life-long mission advocating simple, noiseless toys that don't leave immovable stains or smells behind – the kind that do not bang, bark, bleed or bleep incessantly. So far I have failed miserably in this mission, as each of the children got at least one box with c-o-m-p-l-i-c-a-t-e-d instructions inside.

The other fascinating thing about Christmas Day was, and always is, the food. Why is it we always get offered things to eat that we never eat the rest of the year? Or, in my case, that I never eat? She-who-must-shower-first-in-the-mornings can't eat plum pudding, for example, without brandy butter. I, on the other hand, tend to rush for the toilet with my hand over my mouth at the merest mention of the substance. Put simply, brandy butter must be the most disgusting item on the

Christmas menu and is certainly in my Top Ten of all-time hated foodstuffs. That and cranberry sauce. Not only is it disgusting to eat with turkey meat, but I can't help thinking of all those widowed and orphaned cran-berries that are left behind just to make one measly jar. I like butter and I like jam but I happen to like them in their proper place, like on bread, not on turkey and pud, thank you very much.

We also had a rake of "tibity" plays in the lead up to the big day last week. A tibity play is Number Three's description of what most of us call nativity plays. It was pretty hard having a nativity play and trying to respect Bren the Bishop's order not to "produce" Baby Jesus before Christmas Eve. We did it anyway, but I hope no-body will tell him. Number Three was an angel in her play. Seriously.

Speaking of cribs, when I was in full-time paid em-ployment, as opposed to being the full-time homemaker, nurturer and burner of Christmas puds that I am now, I used to work with a guy who was known as the Moving Crib. But I'm getting distracted here. Number Two and Number Three's tibity play was based around the Spice Grannies. I could explain how this worked, if I had half a day to spare. But I don't. Happy New Year.

*

I decided to buy myself a little something for Christmas. When I tell you what it is, I do not want people running off thinking that I'm changing what I foolishly refer to as my lifestyle. No, it's just something I intend to use very, very occasionally, that's all.

I went into Roches and bought myself a golf putting practise hole thingy. You know the gadget I mean. It's green and it looks like an oversize ashtray and you put it on the ground and hit the ball along the carpet and it plops into this thing, if you're lucky.

Do I play golf? No. Do I intend playing golf? No. But I did play my first two full games ever last summer at Arklow Golf Club. I was pretty useless, particularly so when it came to putting. But, seeing as how I might be down that way next summer, I might get the chance to play another two games. And you have to practise otherwise you never get any better at these things, right?

Anyhow, that's not what I'm getting at. I opened it up and showed it to she-who-was-having-a-cool-yule. She looked at it and said in a suspicious tone of voice, "What is that?", as if it was something I was expecting her to wear as part of some kinky plan I had.

"Have a guess," I said.

"I don't know, is it a kitchen appliance or something?"

"Have another guess," I said, the heart and soul of patience.

"Oh, I know. It's a yokey for steaming a head of cabbage in the microwave, isn't it?"

Our house is depending on this woman for its income. Did you know that? Our lives and our destinies are in the hands of a woman who doesn't know a golf putting practise hole thingy when she sees one.

Speaking of steaming, I have discovered the joys of Tupperware. Yes, a few items of this fine, established hand-made plastic stuff made their way into my kitchen this month. I can now do veggies, steamed in the same micro that Mrs Cabbage Head referred to just now, in less than the time it takes to run down to the off-licence and load up on beer. The children are impressed. Not. They still, apart from Number Two, take an awful lot of encouragement to swallow vegetables. Someone must have told them they are poisonous or something. If All Saints or B*Witched would only do a TV ad, similar to the one good old Ronan Keating did with Christmas presents, telling kids that vegetables are the reason they look so good now.

But I've moved away from what I was going to say.

The lady who does the Tupperware asked me the other week if I'd be interested in having a Tupperware party in my house. I'm sorry to say that I chickened out; I said, no way. Coffee mornings are quite enough for me, thank you very much. As is sitting on a PTA committee with all women. As are fund-raising activities with mostly women. As are school collections, ballet classes and Brownies with mostly women. Enough is enough. Am I not a man? Sure, I'm a man! And men don't do Tupperware parties, see?

So, how did the real business go? Well, Santa was very kind to us this year. He brought all the things that the children asked for in their letters. As with last year, Rudolph ate most of the carrot but left a bit of mess. I still can't help thinking of that pal of a pal who has to clean up reindeer pooh every Christmas morning. Thankfully we've never had to experience that. As for Santa, he had his mince pies and his glass of milk. I bet it didn't take him a second to gobble them down and be on his way to all the other houses in the neighbourhood.

Other high points included a lovely carol service with the school, a gorgeous carol service with the Brownies, and we even had a carol service with the church congregation. With all these carol services you'd think I'd know all the carols off by heart. Not a chance of it. I get to "Round John Virgin" in "Silent Night" and I'm making it up after that. With all the others I am also seriously struggling to make it to the end of the first verse. I've been telling the kids it's because I'm so brainy I can't afford to clog up my head with too much unnecessary information. This year they believe me, God bless them. This time next year you can bet it'll be a different story.

*

It's time to make the resolutions. If you haven't done so already, then get out the pen and paper and start right away. Oh, and just because these good intentions only last a month or so is no reason not to make them. Has it ever stopped the people who make grate brushes from making grate brushes? No. Has it ever stopped Liz Taylor from getting married? No. So why should it stop you or me?

So, here goes, my Top Ten Resolutions:

1. I resolve not to stand like a dumb, grazing ox in queues while out shopping and let people jump me. I was in Dunnes before Christmas queuing for ages when they opened a second queue. Everybody who had come in behind me jumped into it and got served before I did. I resolve to kick up an awful fuss if it happens again.

2. I am not going to host a Tupperware party. It's one thing being at home while you-know-who earns all the money. And it's one thing trying to juggle the lives of three children, manage the contents of a fridge, and all the other food cupboards in the house, and still remain sane. But it's another thing entirely hosting a Tupperware party. Men were not created to host Tupperware parties. I'd feel like a sad case desperate to meet women. A coffee morning, maybe.

3. I am not going to get fat again. I have lost a stone, slowly and naturally, thanks to the NuTron diet, and I do not want to put it back on. I like fitting into my trousers. I like fitting into my new cool leather jacket. I like fitting into the car. Added to this resolution is another half of one: to continue baking my own dairy-free bread. Even if I stop eating it, a dozen or so loaves and I'll have the makings of a good rockery in the garden.

4. I am not going to slag off Boyzone. They are younger than I am, they are smarter than I am, they are richer than I am, they are better looking than I am, and they speak a truth that my five-year-old feels she can understand. I will know my place in this re-

gard in future.

5. I am going to take up a night class of some kind. I must improve myself. I was within a hair's breadth of taking up sculpting last year. Well, they called it sculpting, but when you read the small print it was really only clay modelling. They probably don't let you chip away at large blocks of expensive marble until you're at least six months into it. There could be a Michelangelo inside me waiting to get out. Let's all set our Michelangelos free.

6. I am going to devise a system whereby the children all talk in strict rotation. I have spent the past two years listening to my children all talk to me at the one time. I feel like a traffic cop at Spaghetti Junction, if they have traffic cops there. It's not fair on them because I only ever get to pick up half the information they are communicating to me, nor is it fair on me because I only have one brain, more's the pity. I am going to introduce a colour-coded system and, when they have the green light, they can speak; an amber light means they are next in line; and a red one means "shuddup".

7. I resolve to set more time aside this year for my new Delia Smith book. Too much of my cooking is done on the hoof these days, just thrown together without any thought going into it. I've got to get away from the same old Poulet Roti Au Beurre, the same old Epaule D'Agneau Boulangere, and really strike out and do something adventurous and interesting. Delia is being neglected and it's not right. She deserves better.

8. I resolve next year not to forget our wedding anniversary. This will be the hardest one because it isn't until next November, so I'll have to remember to keep this resolution for an awful long time. I just barely got away with forgetting this year and only because she-who-never-forgets-a-thing forgot too.

9. I resolve to get to know my children's clothes better. They complain bitterly when I put the wrong clothes in the wrong drawers. The same applies to their knickers, socks, vests and tights. Which makes this the Bacon McDouble of resolutions.
10. Finally, I resolve to be the calmest, most serene, most understanding, sympathetic, unflappable, endlessly patient, tirelessly devoted, most unbelievably relaxed father that ever wore desert boots.

*

I have June Rodgers and her merry band of panto people to thank for the latest little bit of fun that is keeping my children amused. We went to see the Christmas panto, "Mother Goose", in the Gaiety Theatre the other night. My three little chickens swooned over the Carter Twins and nearly had a canary when the same Miss Rodgers did her version of the Barbie song, a tune that's been played at top volume in our house ever since Santa brought it. But that's not what I'm getting at, see.

What I mean is that every time I want the kids to do something now, no matter how small (it might even just be a request to listen to me), we have to go through this panto routine.

I'll say: "None of you are listening to me. Will you please be quiet and listen to me?"

Number One will say: "Oh, yes, we are."

I, like a fool, will say: "Oh, no, you're not."

All three will shout: "Oh, yes, we are!"

And then they'll fall about laughing as if I'd wanted to play this game all along. They think I'm a gas Dad, but all I really want, all I really, *really* want, is for them to listen to me every now and then. No such luck.

On the other hand, maybe it's no harm they don't listen to me because sometimes when they do listen, they take things too literally.

This week we had to go back to the dentist and get some of the toothy problems fixed up. Number Three skipped it because she's too young. But One and Two had small jobs done. On the way out, Number One complained of having a terrible taste in her mouth, which was full of saliva at the time she mentioned it. Yes, being with children full-time means you come face to face with yuckiness quite regularly.

"Dhad, whouldh yhou mhindh if I shhhpit," she muttered as we got out onto the street.

Personally, I'm a big anti-spitter but I'd no hanky with me. So, as I was looking around for a bin or something for her to spit into, I foolishly said, half-dreamlike, "Okay."

Before you could say, "Hold on 'til I find a spot for you", the child gobbed on the pavement in front of us. Was I morto? I checked all around me in case an anti-spit lobby was forming instantaneously. Then I had to put the child straight.

"Honey," I said, as shocked as I could make my voice sound, "you can't spit on the path like that, somebody could slip on it and break their neck. And it's a really dirty thing to do."

"Sorry, Dad," she said, genuinely sorry, not like most times she says it when she just wants to get back to watching "The Simpsons" and doesn't want any more hassle from Grumpendad.

"That's okay," I said. "Just remember in future to think of other people. You have to spit to the side where people won't see it or walk in it or..."

Before I could finish the sentence, Number One, still walking, turned her head to one side and let out another spit.

"Is that better, Dad?"

There are days when I wonder if I should go back to school and learn how to speak English in such a way that: (a) will be fully understood; and (b) will have no possibility of being interpreted in any other way except the way I mean it to be.

If I was disappointed at my Number One gobbing on the street, it was nothing to my next big let down. Disappointment of the Week came when the girls were taken to see the movie *Spiceworld* by one of the neighbours. I wanted to see *Spiceworld*. I specifically said it to them. Mumsy got to take them to see *George of the Jungle* and I was to see *Spiceworld*. Not that I like the Spice Girls much. I don't even have a favourite among Posh, Ginger, Sporty, Baby and Scary. Although, Posh does have a certain charm about her and Baby does have an alluring vulnerability which, er... Anyway, what was I saying? Oh yes, it's just that, well, you kind of look forward to going to a movie when you're at home all the time. I couldn't very well object in front of the neighbour, so I had to go along with it, but that's the last time any of my boiled fruit cake is going to that house, I can tell you.

BEFORE

AFTER

Chapter Six

Don't ask me how I'm managing; that's too big an assumption to make

The other day a little battery in my house alarm died. I fettled out the dead item and trudged around town to all the electrical shops with the children in tow. Nobody had ever seen a battery this small. They doubted whether I would ever find a place that sells them. I was not happy with this and neither were the children, but for different reasons, obviously.

So I strapped everybody into the car again and home I went to ring up Telecom to ask why they sold alarm systems with batteries that are irreplaceable. No, a calm young lady told me, they do sell the batteries but I would have to drive three quarters of an hour to their nearest centre if I wanted to buy one. They cost £3. She named the only other shop in Dublin which was selling the same lithium battery for £13. There was no choice to be made here. I merely impart the information as it was given to me.

Once more I strapped the children into the car and off we went. On the way we came across roadworks which slowed the traffic so much I could have read Tolstoy's "War and Peace" from cover to cover. When we got to the shop the children were asleep so I had to carry one, and soft-talk two, into the place.

A prim lady at a prim desk looked at me like I was something out of "Schindler's Ark". I told her I wanted a lithium battery.

"I'm sorry, but we don't sell them over the counter," she said politely.

I was about to get down on my hands and knees and say: "That's alright, pass me one under here," but I had a child in my arms.

"Only qualified Telecom engineers are allowed to install those batteries," she said.

"Oh," I said. "Is that a fact?"

"Yes, it is," she said, looking like the cat that got the cream.

"Well, why didn't your person on the phone say that before I put three children into a hot car and drove for forty-five minutes through heavy traffic to get here? Eh?"

"I've no idea. All I know is that only Telecom engineers are supposed to take those batteries out and put those batteries in."

I held out my hand and showed her the battery. She looked horrified. I had obviously broken some very serious Telecom law.

"I wedged it out using a Biro," I said, trying to make her feel even worse. "And I'll tell you something else, I'm not leaving here until I get a battery because my alarm isn't working and I'm going away on a very long trip (a lie) and I have a lot of very valuable things in my house (a bigger lie) and if I'm robbed I'll sue you and Telecom (a total impossibility)."

"Alright," she said, picking up a phone, "but you'll have to have an engineer out to rebalance your system once you put the battery back in."

Within minutes a nice lady came through a door with a little battery. I paid her and left. My alarm works fine and I've never had sight nor sound of an engineer.

The moral of the story? Any man with three car-crazed children is a desperate character. If you encounter one, don't argue with him, just give him whatever it is he wants.

*

I was in Castleblayney last week speaking at a women's seminar about being a stay-at-home Dad. It was organised by the local women's group called "The Blayney Blades". I tried to hint that the word "blades" has certain connotations for men. They explained that it signified "blade" as in "gay blade", i.e. dashing, daring, that kind of thing. It was not meant to bring to mind the sharp, John Wayne Bobbit kind of blade. Once I realised this, I relaxed and said my piece. I had wanted to give them the fly-on-the-wall flavour of being a househusband but there was so much to cover that I never got around to it. Here's one recent day chosen at random.

A friend's car breaks down and she needs me to pick up her two boys, the first at 12.30 p.m., the second at 12.45 p.m. Her first boy doesn't get out at 12.30 p.m. on the dot so I have to leave my Number Three, who gets out at that time too, in Montessori and go straight to pick up her second boy at 12.45 p.m., otherwise he'll be standing at the gate on his own. When I get there my Number One, who isn't due for picking up until 3 p.m., comes out to say she is sick and wants to come home. My Number Two, who normally gets picked up at 12.45 p.m., is going to a friend's house and both she and the friend's mother are totally confused when they see me there. That makes three of us.

I then pick up the other boy and my Number Three, dead late, and we all go home for Billy Roll sandwiches. My friend comes to collect her two boys at 1.30 p.m. and at 2.45 p.m. my two kids are back in the car to collect Number One's pal from drama who is due to come over to play. When I pull the front door after me I realise I've locked myself out. I rant and rave until I remember that the next door neighbour has a key. Thankfully, he is at home. Phew!

We collect Number One's pal, come home, and feed her sandwiches. I have to put a vent cover outside the house and have 30 minutes to do this because Number

Two has to go to gym. I must put this vent cover on right away; otherwise, all sorts of creatures will crawl into my house and chew and gnaw it to bits, or so my fevered imagination tells me. I get out all the drilling gear and then my Number Two is dropped home so I can bring her to gym. She's home five minutes when she cuts her finger on something or other and major blood and tears follow, of a kind that only hugs, kisses and a plaster will cure. I'm putting on the plaster and Number One is hopping around asking me to open the garage door so she can get her bike. Oh, and could I fix her hula hoop, too?

I open the garage, run around the side of the house, finish the vent job, tidy up and lash off again to drop Number Two to gym. I don't realise I've left a window open with the extension lead hanging out. My house alarm is going loopy while I'm driving to gym singing "Old MacDonald's Farm". The police call by and to my neighbour, who is now sick of me; they tour the outside of the house and then they leave. I arrive back and the alarm is going crazy and the security company rings me to say that the alarm is going crazy. Then the police call back. They assure me there's no need to spreadeagle myself over the bonnet of the squad car; they understand that I'm just stupid. I want to confess to something so they'll lock me away and I can get some peace and quiet. They refuse to humour me and, by the time they prise me off the car and leave, it's time to get the dinner ready.

The point, which is something I meant to make to The Blayney Blades, is that this is what it's like being a househusband. And then on really busy days it's hectic.

*

I like a tidy a house as much as the next man, but Number Two's standards of cleanliness would make a sergeant major proud. Her room is like a new pin and she hates when her room-mate, Number Three, messes it up.

If we are having people over to visit she always says: "Make sure they keep the place tidy, Dad."

I have to admit, it's nice up to a point, but things have been taking a turn for the worse.

I spent an hour one night looking for togs and towels which I'd only taken in from the line earlier. I remembered where I'd put them down, but they were nowhere to be seen. I searched everywhere, twice, and I still couldn't find them until I looked in the laundry basket and there they were. Number Two had tidied them away.

The other morning, I left Number Three's clothes out for her to get dressed by herself, which is our latest project. At breakfast I asked her why she was in her bare feet and she said it was because she couldn't find her shoes or socks which I'd just left out minutes earlier. We searched everywhere, high and low, and then it clicked.

Number Two had tidied them away.

The same with the key for the window locks. Couldn't find it. Why? Number Two had tidied it away. And the library books were due back. I looked all over the house; then I got the Three Degrees to look all over the house and we still couldn't find them. Number Two tidied them away so effectively that they're still nowhere to be found.

The local library is getting to know me very well. I'm the one who comes in regularly looking for a three-week extension on the books. It's going to get to the stage where I won't have to actually go into the library at all. I'll just knock on the window and, once they see it's me, they'll automatically give me an extension.

This obsession with everything being tidied away is either going to drive us all batty or else I'm going to raise three of the finest female detectives the Irish police force has ever known. Either way, I am under instruction from she-who-must-be-encouraged-to-bake-cakes to ignore whatever new heights this tidying rises to.

All this occurred in a week when I also discovered that Number Three, who is four years of age soon, is a big Oasis fan. We were at a summer festival where a band was playing an Oasis number.

"Oh, Dad, I love that song," said the child.

In disbelief, I later recounted this to Number One at home who said: "Oh, yeah, she probably thought it was a Boyzone song."

Whichever the case, these bands have to be applauded. How they've managed to get children so young to like their music is a question worthy of a David Attenborough programme. I bet if you went into the maternity wards of the Rotunda or the Coombe or Holles Street Hospitals, four out of five babies could probably sing you a few lines of Oasis' "Wonderwall".

In the same week, every time the sun did manage to shine, the three of them ran around half naked asking me to blow up the paddling pool. It takes about half an hour to blow up this circular, sagging, puncture-riddled piece of plastic. There are three rings needing air and that means three nozzles to which the foot pump has to be attached. By the time it's ready, my leg muscles are usually seizing up.

After one such display of pumping prowess, Number One told me she could remember when I used to blow up the paddling pool with my mouth.

"Is that a fact," I said, hoping her mother didn't over-hear and start getting ideas about finding a younger man.

"Yeah," she said, "every time you'd blow up a ring you'd have to sit down because your head would be spinning."

The child hasn't remembered it properly. When I'd finish blowing up the pool by mouth I used to swing off through the trees to wrestle a few alligators.

*

I live in a house of play. Anywhere I move, I step over a tangle of bodies in the middle of one makey-up game or another. Or else I'm jumping out of the way of a charging gang of children rushing from one room to another. Lately, wherever I turn, there are signs all over the place. On the door of the hot press there's a poster in scrawly handwriting saying: "Colouring Competition." Underneath in brackets it says: "Come to Office for Details." I've searched and searched but I haven't found the office.

On the toilet door there's a fancy sign, again in scrawly handwriting, which says: "Toilettes for Ladies and Gentlemen." Note the French flavour there.

All the bedrooms have "KEEP OUT" signs on them, some small and friendly like you could ignore them and others written BIG and RED so's to indicate that you'd ignore them at your peril.

The one that really puzzled me was the one on the door to the garage which said: "Cabin 2305." What were they doing? As it turned out, they were playing a fun game for all the family called "Titanic". A happy ending, or what?

The paper affixed to the sitting room door reads: "Staff Only." This has to be a joke because I'm the only staff in the house and I never get a chance to go in there and do any sitting.

Finally, there's a sign reading "Restaurant" on the wall of the landing. They pull out a little table here, two of them sit down as diners in a restaurant, while the other one and some pals pretend to be waiters and cooks and all that. She-who-must-be-in-line-for-a-raise-by-now did a double take the other evening when Number Three walked by the kitchen with a silver tray and a toy mobile phone on it. She followed quietly and saw Number Three hand it to one of the "diners" and say, "There's a phone call for you, madam."

The other day there were four children sitting behind one another on the stairs, swaying from side to side.

They were playing at bobsleighing. It was all going great until I started a snowball fight and Number Three got upset. She said that she wasn't able to make proper snowballs because her hands were getting cold. I mean, how real do these games get?

The same child got a great idea the other day when she was out in the taxi that I drive all afternoon. She tends to get her best ideas in the car. Says she: "Dad, can I send my imitations?"

"You mean your invitations?"

"Yeah, my imvitations for my birthday."

"Your birthday isn't until July, honey."

"I know, but can I send out the imvitations now?"

"It's way too early for July."

"When is July?"

"This is January, then there's February, March, April, May, June and July. Then it's your birthday."

"So can we send out the imvitations now?"

Me, through gritted teeth: "No, darling, I said it's too early. People will forget by the time your birthday comes around."

"There's no need to get grumpy."

"I'm sorry. I didn't mean to get grumpy with you."

"So can we send them out tomorrow, then?"

Is there a health farm for parents? I need one badly. I'm suffering from permanent childminder's tension. How do I know? There are little signs. One is not being able to communicate a simple message to a four-year-old. Another is not being able leave the chocolate fudge cake alone. The first chocolate fudge cake of the year has been baked (by she-who-does-it-on-purpose) and is sitting in the kitchen as I write this. It is laughing at me, taunting me, mocking me.

I will hold out. I will resist. I have good reason. The week before last I went down to the local tailor shop to get the trousers of my only suit taken out. The lady behind the counter checked the trousers and then started filling out a little form.

"We'll take them out as far as they'll go," she said.

"Don't you have to, you know, measure me or something?" I asked.

"We'll let them out as far as they'll go," she said again.

"Without even measuring me?"

"As much as they'll go," she repeated, giving me an ice-pick stare.

I bought a Snickers bar to console myself on the way home. I get my best ideas chewing Snickers bars. Why didn't she just call me "Fat Boy" and get it over with? Why waste time trying to spare my feelings?

*

What was it like before kids? You know, that time when you could sleep through the night without interruption? And wake the next morning feeling fresh as a daisy? I found myself reminiscing wistfully of this earlier, hassle-free existence as an "unchilded" person after a very, very wakeful night during the week.

Number One woke from a nightmare and then woke her parents up, too. She couldn't get back to sleep, no matter what she did. This happened three times. I'd just be nodding off and Madonna would have just started begging me to be her agent again. She was trying to revive her singing career, you see. And then the next thing, bam, it's wake up time.

Out of desperation, I agreed to go in and sleep in the child's bed with her until she fell asleep. Big mistake. It is a small bed. I am a big adult. She fidgets like you would not believe. I got an elbow in the eye, in the back and in the chest. The duvet is so small that my feet got cold sticking out at the bottom. When I got my feet covered my shoulders started to freeze. And then, just as I fell asleep, I got a nudge which nearly sent me half way out of the bed.

At breakfast the child told me that she had fallen asleep soon after I had joined her and was dreaming that I was telling her a joke. She thought it was such a good joke that she gave me one of those "go 'way outta that!" nudges in her sleep.

After a night like that one I wasn't fit to do very much the next day in the way of complicated thinking. I found I had to keep everything very simple. No big words and no complex arrangements with other parents. And very simple food. At a stretch Delia Smith, but no way the Roux Brothers. Oh, and lots of rest, reading and watching black and white movies on the TV with a blanket around my legs for extra warmth.

In the old days, a period I like to refer to as BC, or Before Children, I'd have so much energy that I'd do a full day's work, for which I would be paid, unlike housework, for which I'm not. Then I'd play a football match scoring all five winning goals. After that I'd come home and write a novel which would win the Booker Prize. And then, to round off an otherwise ordinary day, I'd go to a nightclub and chat up five former Miss Irelands. How things change.

I put the blame for this turn of events fairly and squarely on the shoulders of Mother Nature. I can vividly remember, with the aid of the most up-to-date total recall techniques, that as a teenager I refused to sign up for the "happy families" programme. I hated kids and never, ever wanted them. That's why I'm convinced that Nature attaches a kind of bungee cord to men. No matter how far you try to run, eventually it pulls you right back to her way of thinking. So here I am, in the middle of my AD (After Dadhood) period, sleepless, haggard and, yes, okay, alright then, if you insist on dragging it out of me, happy.

That's not to say there aren't downsides. The current one is trying to get Number Three to learn to blow her nose. This might not seem like a large problem in the context of Saddam Hussein's chemical weapons or Bill Clinton's women problems or Boris Yeltsin's boozing. But it is the third time around, much like Clinton's efforts to get inside Saddam's palace. It is a mad thing to occupy yourself with, much like Saddam's preoccupation with thinking he's a popular guy with his people. And it's kind of something you stick with even though you know you should leave it alone, much like Boris' fondness for the sauce. Every couple of days I explain all over again to Number Three about blowing air down her nose. She finds it disgusting that humans could even contemplate such an activity. I've told her that everybody does it. It is the only known way of blowing your nose. She, on the other hand, has resolved that she does not wish to be part of a world which condones this kind of activity. Wait'll she's old enough to take in what Saddam, Bill and Boris get up to.

*

I'm going to save up all my pin money. Then I'm going to buy a ticket to Japan and go find the guy who invented Tamagotchi toys. Then I'm going to strangle him.

My two older children are obsessed with the things. Each has an eight-in-one Tamagotchi that their auntie Liz gave them for Christmas. That's eight different animals. A dog, a cat, a dinosaur, a chicken, a caterpillar, a penguin, a frog and an alien.

Number One is on a caterpillar right now and Number Two is on a fat baby chicken. The things bleep all the time when they need to be fed, walked, loved, hugged, and have their poohs wiped up. Even in the middle of the night.

I've banned them from the kitchen table. This was provoked by numerous conversations with the tops of my children's heads. They literally have to be dug out of the things. Number One nearly had a fit when she-who-has-a-low-tolerance-for-noise banned her from taking it to school. They're banned from schools in Japan, so why not here?

But no, Number One had other ideas. All her friends bring them and leave them on the desk with the sound turned off, so why couldn't she? So we had to allow it. It's going to be fun when the caterpillar needs walkies in the middle of Irish class.

The makers of the thing are presumably incredibly rich by now. So maybe they should invest some of their money in a new phrase book. The instructions on the pack probably contain vital information, but it's impossible to understand them.

"Need to pull the gasket off battery cage before gadget will be on."

Or, more importantly: "The inner liquid chip is fragile, must be prevented from tumble."

And my favourite one of all: "It's forbidden to eat, and users must above age of five. Don't be dismounted by kids."

And what about all that nonsense about Tamagotchis teaching children to be responsible and caring and loving? Number Two's first virtual pet was a fish and she was bored with it in a matter of hours.

"I'm going to kill the fish, Dad," she said to me one day.

I thought she meant the real goldfish in the kitchen.

"No way," I said, spreading myself in front of the fish tank with a rolling pin in my hand and a colander on my head.

"Not those fish. This fish," she said, holding up the little computerised codling in her whatsit.

"Oh," I said, taking off my makeshift helmet. "Why are you going to kill the fish?"

"'Cos it's really, really boring."

"No, sweetie, 'be-cause' it's boring. Not ''cos' it's boring."

"Right! Because it's boring."

"But you're supposed to love it and look after it and everything."

"So what? There's seven more to choose from."

With that she took a cocktail stick and stuck it into the back of the gizmo which, I presume, was the computerised equivalent of putting a pillow over the poor fish's head. I couldn't bear to look. But Number Two carried out the execution with chilling calm.

On the subject of Number Two, we had a curious scene last week which would probably have sent the social workers into a tiz if they'd have been in our house at the time. My lot are fascinated with these grotesque squidgy toys that come in goo. You can get a chopped-off finger in see-through goo, or a chopped-off ear in see-through goo, or even an eyeball. Mmmmmm, juicy, juicy! Anyway, we in our house have a finger and an ear in their respective goos.

Number Two decided that it would be great craic to take out the finger and stick into her open fly. There she was running around the house with a pink finger sticking out of her fly, shouting at the top of her voice: "Look, I have a willy!"

Well, we had people visiting at the time and if I were to tell you that I was seriously morto, I would be underestimating it by a zillion percent. All I could do was give a kind of sickly laugh. Did I look sheepish? All I needed was a farmer to come and shear me. I hate it when the kids do that. They must think these things up in revenge when I give out to them. Then they save the ideas until they'll have maximum effect. There's probably a top-secret notebook around the house somewhere containing lots of these horrible plans, just waiting for the right moment to happen. I'm sorry I was ever grumpy. It won't happen again, I promise.

*

Call me old-fashioned, but travelling in the morning rush hour on the DART this week was not my idea of househusband heaven, especially with Number Three who only came up to everybody else's knees in her buggy chair. She was in danger of being suffocated until I lifted her up in my arms.

We were on a trip to Temple Street Children's Hospital for an annual eye check. There is nothing wrong with her eyes and she never misses a trick; but hospitals are old-fashioned like that and insist on doing their own tests.

The hospital always gives me an appointment for nine in the morning, which means I have to be up really early and then stand in a crush of bodies for forty minutes on the Sardine City Express. It is as close to a sauna as you're going to get on a train. Trying to get a coat and jumper off a child while holding her in your arms is nothing short of a circus act.

I got into such a sweat that I got out at Pearse Street by mistake instead of going on to Tara Street, which meant I doubled the amount of buggy pushing to the hospital. When we got there, everything went smoothly and the eyes checked out fine. Number Three was able to pick out all the letters from the other side of a long room. Had the nurse held up a bag of Tayto crisps, the child could have read it from other end of O'Connell Street.

So we set out for home again, stopping off on the way for a bun in Bewley's Cafe. Nothing less than a cream-filled chocolate eclair would do for Her Highness. As for me, I chose a low fat, low cholesterol, low sugar, high moral ground almond bun.

In a fit of overwhelming generosity on the way to the cafe, I'd promised her we would buy a Teletubby poster from the man on Henry Street after her cake. I did this on the basis that the chances of buying her a real Teletubby for Christmas range between nil and zero. Whoever was impressed with elephants' memories obviously never had children. As soon as she was in the buggy after her cake and milk, we went into search mode for the Teletubby poster man.

Does God play these tricks on people or it is purely coincidence? Do you think we found the Teletubby poster man? My feet ached from walking back and forth past the same doorway that he'd been standing in on the way to Bewley's, but there was no sign of him. In the end we had to leave without the poster and I doubt I'm ever going to reclaim my original place in Number Three's affections ever, ever again.

The DART journey home was bliss. It's amazing how much of the city and environs you can see when you don't have five sets of hairy nostrils ringed around your face. When we got off, at the right stop this time, I had about twenty-five minutes to spare before my first school collection. I toyed with browsing in a book shop or buying those odds and ends which would save me immense hassle later in the afternoon, but when I got into the car I realised I'd put the lock bar on but had brought the set of car keys that did not include the lock bar key.

In a sweat I squidged the lock bar off the clutch pedal and made a pathetic attempt to drive away with the thing still attached to the steering wheel. Remember what Vinny Jones did to Paul Gascoigne in a match years ago? Well that's what the lock bar nearly did to me. I think I got all of five feet from the curb when I gave up on the idea and bundled Number Three into her buggy again. I got home, got the keys, and force-marched all the way back to the car. Time elapsed? Twenty-four-and-a-half minutes. When I arrived to collect Number Two, she asked: "Why were you late, Dad?"

"Things didn't go exactly as I'd planned," I muttered, biting my bottom lip and gripping the steering wheel so hard that my knuckles went white.

*

I'll tell you the kind of week it was: it was the kind of week in which I'd have been better off not trying to be the perfect Dad. I'd organised for Number Three to visit a pal after playschool. With two others to ferry about, this kind of thing always takes a bit of organising. But, no applause please, I go out of my way to provide these little extras.

I turned up at the appointed time to collect "the little cutey with the mind of her own", but was she glad to see her old Dad? Absolutely not. What did she do as her old Dad tried to laugh off her Vesuvius-like temper at being asked to put on her shoes and come home? In front of the little pal and the little pal's mother, she comes up to old Dad's knee and whacks him between the legs with her little Steve Collins fist.

Men will know the pain of this experience. It induces nausea. It scrambles one's thought processes. It brings tears to one's eyes. The mother of the little pal pretended not to notice that my voice had risen an octave. God bless her. It's best if everybody carries on as though nothing happened.

But I'm sure she felt a twinge of sympathy for me as I lurched like a lovesick gorilla back to the car, doubled up in agony.

A couple of days later, I took the terrible tot to the shops. I needed wholemeal and bread soda for the brown bread I was making. In a moment of unrestrained love for the little blonde one, I told her she was the best little thing in the whole world. You're supposed to do this when you're a stay-at-home dad, all the books say so.

Without batting an eyelid, and with a fiendish grin, she said at the top of her voice: "KISS MY BUM."

Old women looked around to see what vulgar child had said it. The shopkeeper dropped a tin of peas he was stacking. As for me, a veteran of many seriously embarrassing encounters, I simply turned on my heel and pretended she belonged to someone else. For the required sixty seconds it takes people to lose interest, I became engrossed in some Irish Breeze anti-bacterial moisturising handwash (ideal for use in the kitchen, pH balanced, gentle on hands).

Then, just the other night, exhausted but feeling good about the world in general, I went in to join them watching "Star Trek: Deep Space Nine". As I settled on the couch, I couldn't help remarking out loud how nice it was to be with them, all together and cosy.

"SSSSSHHHHHHHHHH," was all I got from them. Not a glance, not a loving gesture, not a hug, nothing.

Lesson of the week: feeling loving and mushy? Try next door!

*

Five days a week I wake my lot at 7.15 a.m. It is not a pretty sight. There are mumbles and groans and complaints. The most popular one is: "It's too early, Dad!" It's not as if they are up all night playing. I'm hounding them into bed from about half past eight to make sure they get enough sleep. Still, the next morning it's like trying to deal with three sacks of potatoes. Usually I have to make two trips around the beds to get them into a semi-conscious state.

When it comes to Saturday, it's a different story. The same three sacks of potatoes are suddenly bursting with life at the time I normally can't wake them for school. When I'm trying to have my lie-in, they want to play. When I'm just about to have my last dream, they provide an unwanted wake up call.

Have the Davids Bellamy or Attenborough checked into this? Why is it impossible to get children out of bed from Monday to Friday and impossible to keep them in bed on Saturday and Sunday? I do not like it. Especially when they come in and sit on my belly.

I've suggested to she-who-would-sleep-through-anearthquake that we lock the door and put up some barbed wire. She can't figure out what my problem is. Besides, she says it would be an example of bad parenting. I think she's too soft on them. They must be kept out of my bedroom at the weekends at all costs. My sleep is worth more to me than some namby-pamby definition of parenting.

I suppose I'll have to put up with it. They say revenge is a dish best served cold. When they're all teenagers and going to discos I'll be in their bedrooms at dawn on weekends, putting up shelves or painting wardrobes or practising the violin. When they ask through bleary eyes what in the name of God I'm doing, I'll say: "It's payback time!"

Another thing I noticed this week was that they are also pretty bad at remembering rules. Every day I have to remind them two or three times of the little agreements we have that ensure the smooth running of the household. Every house needs rules. The world needs rules. If there were no rules people could do what they liked. Ask Bill Clinton. So we have rules about the little jobs they have to do.

We have a roster for clearing the breakfast things away, and for setting the table for dinner in the evenings. We have a rule about each of them clearing away their own dinner plate; about not leaving dirty clothes on their bedroom floors; about taking shoes off when they come into the house; about teasing each other. And we have a rule about slapping, hitting, spitting and biting. They are not allowed do any of these things to me.

But do they remember? On rainy days they've usually burst into the house and reached the sitting room before I rugby tackle them and get their shoes off. Once they've finished their dinner it's like they have ants in their pants because they're at the door before I lasso them and get them back to clear away their plates. As for our roster for setting tables, it's as if we were playing a kiddie version of "Blankety Blank" every single day. When asked whose turn it is, they look at each other as if the answer is on the tip of their tongues but they just can't think of it. My instinct is to let it go and do the job myself, except I know that this is exactly what the little con artists want. Unless I persevere, they'd work it so they never have to lift a finger around the place. Having said that, of course, they are the best. Not that you needed to be told that but I thought I'd mention it, just in case.

So, to the real business. The NuTron people told me to expect headaches on the first week and, boy, did I get headaches. That's a sign it's working, the young dietician lady told me cheerfully. I am down three pounds. The headaches mean my body is learning to live without cakes, biscuits, chocolate and pizzas. It is a painful lesson. I've also developed a twitch in my face but I'm sure it'll go away. Come to think of it, it started right after I'd tried to eat a soya-based yoghurt. Never try to do this at home on your own. At least not without a basin on your lap.

*

Things have certainly got off to a fine start. I nearly broke my neck on Number Three's Barbie doll in the shower. Barbie has to have her hair washed every now and again, you see, but she never gets put back in the place she is supposed to live. She just lies on the floor of the shower with no clothes on, the shameless hussy.

This came at a time soon after I had managed to evict the previous inhabitants from my precious shower. A family of rubber ducks lived in the shower before Barbie arrived. These were Number Three's favourite ducks who had been nesting there for far too long, since September, if memory serves me correctly. I couldn't move without tripping over one of these things. It was quacking me up (sorry, I couldn't resist that). When I eventually asked her to move them there was such grumbling and moaning you'd think I was asking her to put them out onto the street without a roof over their roundy yellow heads. Now Barbie lives there instead.

This is part of a bigger problem, though. It might be the smallest room in the house but there is no peace and quiet to be had there. As soon as any of them hear that door closing, they are in there with me, asking me questions, seeing if I'll do their hair, wondering what time their mother will be home, asking to watch television, eat sweets, go to McDonalds, get a puppy, build a go-kart, you name it. Where I come from, one's ablutions are a sacred and private matter. The world might be ending but you mustn't disturb the process that goes on in that most holy of holy spaces.

Not so to my lot. They see it as an opportunity to catch their Dad at his weakest moment. The way they see it, I might want them to go away so much that I'm likely to agree to anything. It's an old Gestapo trick that they have obviously picked up from somewhere. I am not going to speculate exactly where, or from whom, because it might lead to divorce.

For a while I thought they were over this habit. They had stopped doing it over the Christmas holiday period completely, I suppose because there was so much other stuff to occupy them. But Buckaroo is totally bucked now, the Walkmans are footsore, the inflatable sofa is just so much hot air in pink plastic, the Boyzone CD is much the same, and now they're coming back to me to entertain them.

I need a new rule about this. I know I should have added it to my list of New Year's Resolutions but, hey, I just can't think that fast, alright? The new rule is going to be that when father is in the little room, either showering or doing anything else, he must not be disturbed. Whosoever shall disturb him by either walking in on top of him, knocking repeatedly on the door, shouting questions through said door, or running their fingernails up and down the outside of the door in a way that sets his teeth on edge shall have a terrible vengeance wreaked upon them. They shall either: (a) miss the first five minutes of "The Simpsons" for the next three episodes; (b) not be allowed a Big Mac on the next visit to McD's and be given only the plain, piddly burger instead; or (c) be in charge of the hot press for a week. None of which, if imposed, will make them happy campers.

Number Two wasn't a very happy camper either when she heard of a bank robbery on the radio. The thought of armed gangs roaming around the countryside trying to steal other people's money just sets her thinking about all sorts of nasty possibilities.

"I hope they don't rob my bank," she said.

I hadn't the heart to tell her that her money was in the Post Office and not the bank, mainly because it would have meant facing a long and torturous explanation about the difference between the two types of savings institutions. The child is an angel, saving every penny she gets, which is a trait she has not inherited from either her mother or her father. I suspect she's watched us spend every penny we have and has vowed never to turn out like that when she grows up. As far as robbers are concerned, I've told her not to worry about baddies like that because the police always catch them and throw them in jail.

I wonder if now is a good time to ask her for a loan?

Chapter Seven

Housework has a reputation for being boring and unrewarding but that's overselling it a little

A survey tells me that only 17 out of every 1,000 men are stay-at-home dads. That's 0.017% of the male population, which is tiny.

Do they want to know why? I'll tell them: because the accessories are terrible. Everything that a man is supposed to use to keep the house clean or do the laundry or cook the meals is designed for a woman. And men just won't stay at home if they have to use womanly things.

So here's my solution. Let's get a whole new range of man things out there so that guys like me can feel cool doing the housework.

For example, why can't someone invent a special belt – leather, of course – that will carry all the tools of the trade? Like those carpenters you see on building sites. I'd like one that could hold the Windolene and the Jif and the Mr Sheen, as well as a duster or two.

It's hard to explain this need to women because it's just a man thing that goes right back to when we used to strap on six guns to play cowboys. Same difference, only now we could swagger around the house and beat the bluebottles to a draw or hum and haw over difficult stains on the carpet the way builders do when they're looking into a serious hole.

The same with cleaning out the fireplace. I ask you, what man wants to do this with a little bitty brush whose head keeps falling off and that was obviously invented in order to drive sane people mad? Eh?

No. What men at home need is some great, big suction machine that needs lugging into the sitting room and has a special, knacky way of being started up that women can't master and that requires tons of muscle just to manoeuvre it half an inch to the left.

This is what I'm talking about – man things. By the way, anybody out there thinking of putting these ideas into production should be aware that I will require at least 20% of all profits.

Now, where was I? Oh, yes, and the same with rubber gloves. You want to buy heavy-duty rubber gloves? Well, you can have any colour you like, so long as it's black!

Suppose I'm in a businesslike mood one day. Can I choose pin-strip gloves? No way. Or suppose it's summer time and I'm feeling gay. Can I reach for the bright red heavy-duty gloves? No way. Black is all you get.

There is so little imagination going into household products these days that it's a scandal worthy of a government tribunal of enquiry. Call in the manufacturers, put them on the spot and let's get some answers to these very important questions.

The other day I was in the kitchen and I noticed the linoleum needed cleaning. What did I have to do? Get out the mop, the bucket and the Flash. Why has nobody invented kitchen-floor-cleaner-slippers? Eh? Just slip 'em on, slide around the floor while you cook and, hey presto, instant shine. I don't know, sometimes I think the people with all the brains are at home raising kids.

*

Fellow househusbands out there will understand this: it's been such great drying weather lately that I've had to go out and buy another lorry-load of clothes pegs. But while thinking I was solving a problem, I created another, because I put so much laundry on the whirligig line that none of it dried out properly. Isn't life a bitch?

Whirligig lines must have been invented by architects because they're a great idea, they look really good and they don't work. Speaking of washing clothes leads me to my next observation. I am putting on a wash every single day of the week. My life is controlled by the washing machine. It is such a part of my life that when I go out for a quiet meal at the weekends it should come with me instead of my wife.

So, to correct this situation, I had a brainwave. I decided a little while ago that I was going to try and get the children to keep their clothes clean; you know, get more than one day's wear out of them.

Was I stupid? Was I the most naïve man in the entire universe?

I am convinced the two older ones slide around on their backsides and their bellies from the moment I leave them to school to the time I collect them again. If the youngest one can get past breakfast without major staining of her clothes, then I know it will be a good day and I generally choose that day to buy my lottery ticket.

Which leads me directly to my third observation of the week. I have spent so much time at the washing line that my bald head now sports a roaring red suntan. I'm sure Rupert Murdoch's satellite can pick up my ultraviolet throbbings as soon as I step out of the back door. Ordinarily a suntan is a problem for me because people in vegetable shops keep feeling my head to see if I'm ripe, but now I realise it is of huge benefit because when I'm out for a drink people think I got the tan down in the Med and they assume I must be filthy rich to be able to afford a holiday at this time of year. Pretty cool, huh?

But, of course, we're not filthy rich, or rich; just filthy, as is the case with the children's clothes. It's even worse when they are not at school. The other week we took them for a picnic to some woods in Wicklow. After just 2.5 seconds in the place they looked like Army rangers on manoeuvres, complete with grimy clothes, smudged faces and the eyes of trained killers. After an hour or so I lassoed them and hauled them back to the car.

Not long after we'd driven off, we passed a hearse without a coffin. Number One was mighty impressed at this.

"What does that silver sign in the back of the hearse say?" she asked her mother.

"It says 'Flannery and Sons'," her mother replied.

There was silence in the back of the car for a while. And then came the sound of muffled sobbing.

"His sons as well," she sniffled, horrified at how cruel life can be.

I passed back a spotless, magnificently ironed, white hanky and wished it a quick and painless death.

*

Let's clear the air on something first. When I am in the supermarket I look a sight. I admit it. I have nothing to hide. I slob around in clothes that are hanging off me, my bald head and double chin making for quite a fleshy vision. But I am not the worst thing you are going to find down the cereals aisle.

This week I was swishing around to the music of Rod Stewart when suddenly my lungs seized up and my voice disappeared. Some heavily made-up woman was wearing a perfume that was so strong there was a sprawl of comatose shelf-packers behind her. I'd have said something to her myself only by the time they brought me 'round she'd already passed through the checkouts and left the girls slumped over their tills.

A little later, when my sight had fully returned, I noticed an extraordinarily happy middle-aged man, humming and singing to himself and letting out a big

"Ahh" every time he found what he was looking for. I hid behind things in order to get a good look at what he was up to. Nobody can be that happy in a supermarket. I know; I am a veteran. I have three stripes on my arm, one for each kid that I have to take with me. I swaggered away and left him in his innocence. He was obviously new to this game but he'd learn.

Further on there was a bit of a trolley jam and I had to edge past a round lady, rounder than me even, who was wearing leggings designed for a greyhound. She lost her balance slightly and crushed me up against the tinned pineapples. I came out alive, though, just a cracked rib or two, nothing serious. A guy can't show pain in a supermarket.

Then, at the household section, something caught my eye and it was love at first sight. It was a bright red Vileda Supermop and I felt that I just had to have it. Have you seen it? It is the mop of mops and only £7! I wanted it so much that I had to walk away. I told myself it was an extravagance I couldn't afford, until I saw Happy Harry come around the corner with one sticking out of his trolley. I ran straight back and was about to buy my very own Vileda when I noticed Spontex had one for £5, and with a refill mop head, too.

I hang my head in shame as I write this, which is a bloody awkward way to write, but I bought the Spontex one because it was, well, dammit, because it was cheaper. Yes, cheaper – you've read it right. I sold out on something I really wanted for a measly two pounds. Every now and then, when the sun is going down, or when Daniel O'Donnell is singing on the radio, I think of that gleaming red Vileda and I imagine all the things we could have done together. But don't feel sorry for me. I knew what I was getting into when I quit my job. Nobody said it was going to be a picnic.

*

A grey cloud hangs over our house. What was once a happy place, chiming to the sound of children's laughter, is now filled with wailing and gnashing of teeth and the picking of scabby bits. Why? Because my housekeeping skills have been found wanting.

She-who-lives-life-at-90-miles-an-hour came in the other night and the place was a mess. I stammered out an explanation about writing in the mornings and ferrying kids in the afternoons. But it was no good. The facts are the facts are the facts. The place was a mess.

As she strode to the bedroom, one of Number Three's socks stared out at her from the corner of a shelf. Number Three takes her clothes off quite vigorously every night; that's where the sock landed and that's where it stayed. We've no idea how long it was there but Trinity College is carbon dating it right now.

Then she went into Number Two's bedroom and had to wade across the floor through a sea of debris. Number Two is normally the tidiest child in the universe but this week she's been going through that "teenage rebel" phase ten years before it's due. Clothes, toys, books, shoes, bedclothes, pyjamas, jewellery – you name it, it was on the floor. She called me in to look at what she was seeing, but when I went in I couldn't see her for the mess.

"Where are you?" I called out.

"I'm behind teddy bear mountain," came the reply.

I tried explaining that I hadn't been in the room all day but it was no use. The facts are the facts are the facts.

It's been pretty much the same story all week. Old newspapers and bags full of kitchen rubbish were blocking the back door one day. That didn't bring any cheer into her life. Then there was an empty toilet roll on the holder for three days in a row. I hate that, don't you?

Oh, and I nearly forgot, the carrot soup that was lovingly made for me and the children last weekend, and which I'd only got around to putting in the freezer on

Wednesday, came out of the freezer on Friday smelling incredibly whiffy.

My hands are in the air. May I make a last request?

A lady informed me recently that she reads my newspaper column and she reckons I'm a parent under stress. I agree. She says anybody who keeps forgetting as many things as I do has to be under stress. I agree. She reckons I need somebody in to help me. I agree. Maybe to do the cooking and cleaning and ferry the kids around and help them with their homework and make their tea and bathe them and put them to bed. I couldn't agree more.

To this end I'm going to double my lottery spend to £2 a week. I am also going to pray a lot more and be nicer to children, including my own, and small animals.

That same lady reader will probably be appalled to know that I forgot to bring my friend Sinead's son home from school on Thursday. I'd brought him in with my three in the morning and that went smoothly enough. At lunch time I went to collect him and told him in the playground that I was bringing him home. Then I started talking about PTA stuff with the PTA parents. Then I chewed the fat with the other househusband, you know the kind of thing, swapping recipes, bitching about the price of new shoes for the kids. Then I promptly went home and forgot poor Seany. Luckily, Nicola, who is Emily's mother, was going the same way and took him home.

Yes, indeed, it's been that kind of week. To make amends I decided I was going to get more disciplined with myself and with the children generally. Order and cleanliness were to be the new rules in our house. I started by helping Number One rearrange and tidy her bedroom, even dishing out a pretty neat tip on how to clean her floorboards. That evening, she-who-can-even-swim-faster-than-me went to praise the work. She skidded around the floor in her stocking feet and Number

One went head over heels. Telling the child to use Mr Sheen to clean floorboards was, I have since been informed, probably the silliest thing I've done since the time I served up tuna sandwiches while the children were watching *Flipper*.

*

At last, spring is here. My favourite time of year. Time to dust out the old cobwebs. Time to make that special effort to bring the Christmas tree to the dump. Time to find those unpaid bills in the pile that got filed under "c" for "chaos" last November. I'm a firm believer that winter time is for hibernatin' but not for doing things.

We're out of it now, though, so there's no excuse. It's time to get up and do things. The days are getting longer and the clock goes forward pretty soon. Why, even St Patrick's Day is behind us. No more green "Shamrock Shakes" at McDonalds. The kids went for them in a big way – until the first taste and then it was: "Yeeuucchh, it's minty!!" and I had to go back and buy them drinks they could drink.

Spring time means DIY in our house. I went to Woodies with Number Two to get myself a 20mm drill bit. I was going to do some serious drilling. Put air vents in the bedrooms. I like air in the bedrooms. It's an old-fashioned notion, having oxygen in your lungs at night – obviously a tradition that went completely over the head of the builder of our house.

So there I was in Woodies. No longer Lasagne Man, but instantly transformed into Builder Dad. Strong, tough, scruffy as hell, smelling slightly of BO and honest-to-God dirt. Then Number Two met a pal and the next thing they were playing hide and seek.

Let me be honest here: Woodies was made for hide and seek. When you're a kid, that is; not when you're an adult. Especially not when you're an adult who wants to get back home and start drilling with his 20mm drill bit. Offhand, I'd say I dropped about ten minutes trying to find Number Two. Eventually I found her in the gardening section but, by that time, tough Builder Dad had been changed back into stressed Blubbering Dad.

On the way home I called into a builder's yard for another vital piece of the DIY jigsaw. The guy behind the counter was very helpful. He could see I was a novice at this game but he didn't laugh once. I explained what I wanted in detail.

"An airbrick, yeah, we have them," he said, trying not to yawn.

"No, no," I said, "what I'm looking for is plastic and about so big and it's red to match the bricks..."

"Yeah," he said, "an airbrick."

"No," I said firmly, because I know how these guys try and sell you anything, "it's not a brick. It's plastic, a red plastic, I suppose because it lasts longer that way, and..."

Before I could finish he leaned over the counter so that our noses were nearly touching. I remember thinking how he looked like Lee Van Cleef because of the way he spoke through his teeth.

"It-is-called-an-airbrick-pal-trust-me-I-know-about-these-things."

"Right, so," I said, noting his bad dental work, "I'll have just the one, please."

When I got home, I set about my manly task of punching big holes in the bedroom wall. Lots of noise and lots of dust. The kind of environment that we househusbands were born to live in.

I felt the satisfaction of breaking through to the other side, knowing that after a few more of these holes the final touch could be put in place. Yes, I'm talking about the matt white "adjustable interior ventilator with integral flyscreen". I couldn't wait.

But when I broke through the wall there was no light coming through from the other side as there should have been. Only darkness. I looked out of the window and, yep, it was still daytime. This was puzzling. It was only when I went outside the house to look that I could see the problem. I'd drilled through the bedroom wall into the chimney breast. Thank God for Polyfilla, is all I can say.

Maybe it's still a little early to be getting into DIY. I think I'll kick back, as the Yanks say, and wait a few months. Don't want to strain myself. Don't want to peak too soon.

*

I have stumbled upon an important discovery. Like all great discoveries it is blindingly simple, but amazingly effective. After constant, and at times thankless, research I have at last cracked the problem of our messy hot press. Where there was once an open space into which everything was dumped willy-nilly, I now have order. The answer to my problem came in the unlikely shape of five empty shoe boxes, one for each of us. No more the large mound of intertwined socks and panties. No more the long hours of disentangling my smalls from every-body else's. Now it is as simple as taking out a box and knowing, with 90% certainty, that what's inside belongs to the person whose name is on the box. And the joy of it all is that I thought the idea up myself, all on my own. I was going to throw a party but it's too soon after Christmas so I'll probably save the celebration for nearer the summer.

It's not quite a 100% foolproof system yet, though. The reason is that, on the sorting end of things, I'm still a bit shaky. I mean, I know my own undies inside out, so to speak. It's just that I get everybody else's a bit mixed up at times. Especially if they've all had new stuff bought for them at the same time. It leaves me so confused that I end up making guesses as to which goes where.

If there is a single common complaint from all of the children that I get as a househusband, leaving aside their picky tastes in food, it is to do with finding the wrong knickers in their drawers, if you follow me. But I have a plan to solve this problem too. From now on, when it is my sorting day I'm going to have one of them beside me at all times acting as a spotter. When they spot me putting the wrong item in the wrong box, her job will be to point it out immediately so that the mistake doesn't travel any further into the system. Otherwise, there's hell to pay at the other end. I've gone to such trouble getting my new shoeboxes into place I want to be sure they work perfectly from now on. I'm getting a warm glow all over just thinking about it.

And speaking of working perfectly, something which is not doing so is our newest goldfish. The old Velvet Pom Pom just doesn't look like he has the legs to go the distance. He's been skulking down the bottom of tank for days now. As I write, I have a phial of tank water in my pocket to take down to the pet shop man so that he can do an analysis to check if there's something in it that doesn't agree with the fish. If the VPP pops his clogs sometime soon, he'll be the second to do so in nearly as many months. The garden is fast becoming a fish graveyard. Personally, I think they die of boredom, but I'm sure there's a million vets who'd disagree with that diagnosis. I had the fatherly task of comforting Number Three, who owns the VPP lock, stock and two flagging fins, when she saw that he wasn't up to playing with the other fish. It was a sad and meaningful moment, for about a nanosecond.

The same child was telling us about her best pal in school the other day. For some reason the discussion came around to the kind of food this pal likes. Number

One is in class with this child's big sister, so she knows the family well. It was she who floated the idea that they didn't eat meat. Number Three said she didn't know whether they did or not. Number One was pretty sure they didn't eat meat.

"They're vegetarians, I think," Number One said.

"No, they're not," said Number Three, "they go to the same church as us."

Finally, everybody with young children will have heard knock-knock jokes until they are coming out their ears. You've also probably noticed that the nearer the jokes are to toilet humour, the louder the children laugh. The joke that follows is Number Two's favourite at the moment and she's only told it to me five times, which shows great restraint and maturity in my view. If you haven't heard it, then feel free to try it out on an under-nine in your life.

"Knock, knock."

"Who's there?"

"Done up."

"Done up who?"

"Well, you'll have to change your trousers then, won't you?"

Ha, ha, ha.

*

Men are supposed to be good at techie things, aren't we? I'm forever telling she-who-works-every-hour-God-sends to read the manuals. Time the video to tape a TV programme? I have to do it. Tune in and pre-set the radio stations on the stereo? I have to do it. Unravel the mysteries of the answering machine? I have to do it.

Just so she'd have a colourful record of my high-blood pressure face in years to come, I bought her a camera for Christmas. It's one of those new ones with the dinky little roll of film that you just slot in and the camera does the rest. I read the manual from cover to cover and urged her to do likewise, which she never did.

Despite this, things went swimmingly and, when we got the prints back from the photo shop, lo and behold, we also received a new film with each set. At this rate, I greedily thought to myself, I'll never have to buy film for this gizmo ever again. Life was unbelievably good.

And then disaster struck. The camera wouldn't work. It appeared to be very, very sick. Not a blink out of it, nor even a half-hearted flash. I wouldn't have minded so much except that I'd just loaded a new film with forty exposures on it. So I went back to the shop. I had to be firm with them. The camera was only two months old. It shouldn't just clap out like this. This was a reputable shop and a reputable brand of camera. They got the message.

A few weeks later, after the emergency response team had pored over the thing and discovered there was nothing wrong with it, the camera was ready. She-who-has-a-detective's-mind collected it. The guy in the shop told her that the only thing that might possibly have caused the problem was that someone had loaded a used film.

"A used film," I echoed in surprise.

"Yes," she said. "They sent us back the used film with the prints. It has the negatives on it."

"Is that a fact," I said, all ears.

"Yes, and if you load it in, the camera thinks you're a big eejit and it won't work for you."

"Well," says I, "aren't them cameras the cleverest things."

"Yes, they are. But," she added, "you'd have known this 'cos you always read the manuals."

"To be sure," I said, "only a big eejit of a dope would do something as stupid as the likes of that."

Moving quickly on, Number Three has had her second flu in a matter of weeks. It's just not fair. I was invited to a fab coffee morning during the week and I

had to cancel out because the child needed lots of TLC.
All the girls were going to be there. But that's what happens with children, isn't it? Still, there'll be other coffee
mornings. They won't be as good as that one, mind you.
That was probably going to be the best of the season.
But I suppose I'll just have to try and be mature about
it.

Oh, and the milk situation got worse. Remember I
mentioned how the abolition of glass milk bottles was all
part of a sinister plot to sell more milk (because the kids
spill half the milk trying to get the square cartons open)?
Well, that was only half the story.

The other half of this plot is that it's impossible to
cancel the milk now. I went out the other night with a
"No Milk Today – Thank You" note. But where was I to
stick it? In an empty carton? Do you get my point? Empty
milk bottles were ideal for putting the cancellation note
in. You can't do this with cartons. And if I can't cancel
the milk, then things will get serious. As it is, I have so
much milk that the house looks like a supermarket. How
many others suffer as I do?

Luckily, I found six empty milk bottles that've been
sitting in a battered old carry crate we inherited from
the last owner of the house. It's sad, really. The milkman
has ignored them from the day glass bottles were phased
out. I put my cancel note in one of them and went to bed
feeling happier in myself. The next morning, not only
was my milk not cancelled but I got twice my normal
order plus a half dozen eggs, three of which broke
because the egg box fell as I was lifting everything into
the house. The guy doesn't see glass; he doesn't hear
glass; he doesn't speak glass. Don't anybody tell me
that being at home is easy.

*

I have a deep suspicion that my three little girls are not

mine. Oh sure, I'm the biological father alright, the one chosen at random by nature to perform the reproductive act. But it goes much deeper than that. I suspect that my girls are actually reincarnations of Pharaoh's daughters.

I first became alerted to this possibility last summer when we were at the beach. Instead of wanting to make sandcastles, the children opted to build a pyramid. When I suggested that, for a bit of fun, they bury me, Number Two jumped up and said without a hint of humour: "Okay, I'll get the bandages."

Things have got steadily worse since then. Now at mealtimes they insist that I cut every millimetre of fat off their meat. If one scintilla enters their mouths it is immediately spat back out with much gesturing and protesting. If I offer them a pizza, it has to be inspected most carefully and any piece of vegetable matter, such as a mushroom or a green pepper or a sliver of onion, must be removed instantly. The Pharaohs always were picky about their food.

There is a similar ritual at bath time. The water temperature must be exactly right otherwise they will not entertain "bathing", as they call it for some strange reason. When the soaping and shampooing begins, the unspoken rule is that no water or soap or shampoo must enter their eyes. Judging by what I've experienced, I can only assume that failure to adhere to this rule must have spelled instant death for housemaids in ancient Egypt.

Another curious feature is their inability or unwillingness, it's hard to tell which, to carry anything with their own hands. If we are shopping and I ask one of them to carry a light bag, the look says it all. I can tell they hate me because I am not rich enough to afford servants to perform these menial tasks.

They seem to be able to communicate by mental telepathy. I was giving out to the youngest one the other day for smearing yoghurt over the couch when I became aware of the other two standing beside me, staring at me. The scene was straight out of *Village of the Damned*, that 1960 black-and-white movie.

"She's only three, Dad," they said together, calmly.

"I know, but there's yoghurt all over..." I stuttered.

"You're not to shout," they warned.

"But I've got to clean..."

"It was an accident," they repeated firmly, arms around the juvenile offender. "Wasn't it?"

"Yes," I said, feeling suddenly tired, "it was... an accident."

My research tells me that Nefertiti, the Pharaoh's wife, had six daughters. This means that someone else out there has the other three. God love you pal, I know how it is.

Chapter Eight

You could call this the entertainment section, if you have a warped sense of humour

Migueletto, the clown, looked at me so closely that I thought his red nose was going to touch me. Out of politeness I looked away until he'd moved on – except that when I turned back he was still there and this time he had a big smile on his face. Then the full horror of what he was up to struck me.

I had foolishly decided to take not just my own children but also four others along to Duffy's circus.

Equally foolishly, I had sat them all in the front row of the cheap seats, to make it easy for the supplies of candy floss and popcorn to get through.

Even more foolishly, I had dumbly nodded my head when Migueletto asked me if I'd step into the ring for a moment.

Never, ever, ever, *ever* do this. Just say no. Plenty of other parents did just that later on but, oh no, not me. I had to nod my big head and agree. Talk about the Worzel Gummidge of the parenting world. If Mr Bean ever decides to try out a double act, then here I am.

All I could hear was the laughter of my seven, and the two hundred or so other kids in the place, as I was led off by a very small Mexican wearing gaudy clothes and face paint to participate in a game they play at circuses called "The Humiliation of Fathers".

Migueletto had a really special version lined up for me. I was to be a tiger, no less. I had to sit on a stool in the middle of the ring, hold my paws up in front of me like a good tiger and do some roaring.

"He's no tiger," said Mr Duffy, the ringmaster, over the microphone, "he doesn't have enough hair."

Ha, ha, ha, laughed the whole tent. Wasn't this hilarious fun? Wasn't this the most fun way of spending a weekday afternoon?

NOT!

To compensate for my lack of hair, Migueletto threw a tatty leopard-skin scarf over my head. If that scarf could've talked, it would have had some stories to tell. But I couldn't allow myself get distracted by that because I had to concentrate. This time Migueletto wanted me to lift my legs off the ground, which I did, and the audience applauded.

For my grand finale, he said I was going to jump through fire. It seemed reasonable to me. After the pain of what I'd just been through, second degree burns from jumping through a blazing hoop weren't going to add much more to my discomfort.

He led me to the side of the ring where I stood up on the edge. He begged the audience to be quiet because this was a very dangerous act. Then, disregarding his own safety and mine, he held a cigarette lighter at my feet and urged me to jump over it for all I was worth.

I felt queasy at the thought of what could happen if I didn't get this right. But with seven children hanging on my every movement, I knew I couldn't show fear. I jumped and before I knew it, it was all over and I was safely back on firm ground again.

Amid much clapping and cheering, I returned to my seat and tried to regain my senses. The next hour or so was a bit of a blur, such was the effect it had on me. Even Heidi and her performing goats and dogs are just a dim memory now.

Spiderman finished the show with an aerial display on the high wire. As a final stunt, he pretended to fall off the swinging bar he was standing on. He was wearing special boots which were attached to the damn thing, but nobody told me that. I thought he was a goner for sure and my nerves couldn't stand any more.

Next thing I remember, the eldest was splashing water in my face trying to bring me around. I was mumbling and it wasn't a pretty sight: "Circuses. Doncha love 'em. Can any of you kids drive? Where's the exit? I need a drink."

*

What is it with me and circuses? All I want to do is go along and be anonymous, one of the crowd. Instead I am like a beacon for clowns. I must give off a smell that attracts them. Maybe they can see the fear in my eyes.

We all went to the American three-ring circus this week. Not only was the place like a mangrove swamp because of all the rain but a clown called Buttons made a beeline for me just five minutes into the show. He asked if I'd throw a floppy ring to him. Two words came to mind but I couldn't say them because children were present. So I threw it and was applauded. Then he wanted me to do it again, except this time he went to the far side of the tent. I tried my best but it landed about a hundred yards short of where he was standing. So funny Buttons made this big deal about how weak I was and what a pathetic throw it had been and everybody laughed. Ha, ha. Then he came back to me and, for our big finale, we threw it back and forth about, oh, two hundred times.

So the show went on, and a good show it was too, with lions and tigers and elephants and a trapeze artist called Lorraine whose costume consisted of a piece of string elaborately festooned with shimmering sequins. To be honest I didn't know whether to look up or look away.

At the interval the children sat on an elephant and had their picture taken. The elephant was more interested in snatching the candy floss I was minding for his passengers than posing for the picture. Didn't he know that this photo would be important in years to come? Don't they train these animals any more? Then the girls all had a bouncy ride around the ring on a Shetland pony.

On the basis that lightning never strikes twice, I settled down to enjoy the second part of the show. No sooner had a Hercules lookalike finished balancing on a stack of rolling pipe-ends while swinging on a spaceship suspended from the roof, than the curse of the clowns struck again. Over came this little bas..., er, clown, called Chico. He grabbed me and an older man and took us into the middle of the ring. We had to hold a tray on which there was a little plastic milk bottle cap and play blow football with it. Which we did. I scored a great goal. Then Chico put blindfolds on us and we had to do it again. At the whistle we blew like crazy only to discover that we were blowing talcum powder all over each other. Ha, ha, ha. I laughed so much I nearly had to go for surgery to get the smile off my face.

Near the end of the show, these two ponytailed Italian gentlemen came out and did some very dangerous stunts on a steel contraption that looked like a giant hamster wheel attached to a windmill. Not content with that, one of them then decided to do it blindfolded. What is it with these people and blindfolds?

And guess who had to check if the blindfold was really a blindfold? I got a black hood put over my head. Inside it there was no air and it smelled of hair oil.

"Sir, you can tell me, ees eet a blindfold?"

I shook my head from side to side instead of nodding up and down but, no matter, this was the circus and I was now part clown. He took the hood off and I started to breathe again.

"But you must test the other side," he said, happily putting the hood back on me. I held my breath, nodded my head, and he took it off again.

"Eet ees a blindfold, yes? You could not see me, yes?"

I went, "Yes, yes, yes," as a way of encouraging him to get on with the bloody show. He rubbed my bald head as if he'd never seen one before and ran off to finish his act. For the grand finale, the Viennettas stunned us all with triple backflip somersaults on the trapeze and after that we went home.

If I ever go to a circus again, which might be never, I'm going to wear a wig and a moustache. Obviously these people have a photo of me filed away somewhere, under "p" for "patsy", and they pass it around from circus to circus.

*

The children needed some culture in their lives so I took them to see the new *Batman* movie. A week later, as an antidote, my wife decided that a night out at the National Concert Hall was needed.

There are some things you must know about going to the Concert Hall with children. First, there is no air-conditioning in the place, so be prepared to fan your youngest child with the programme for near enough to two solid hours. Try and encourage your life partner to share in this activity and do not take "no" for an answer.

Secondly, try and explain to your children before you enter the grand hall that going to see large people with deep voices singing with a big orchestra is not the same thing as going to the cinema. The rest of the audience will not appreciate it when they eat sweets with loud, crinkly paper, nor when the older ones loudly whisper things like "I'm thirsty" or "I'm too hot" repetitively.

Thirdly, and most importantly, do not buy tickets for the choir seats above the orchestra. We did, in the front row. I spent the whole night paranoid because we were facing the entire audience of the NCH. I was probably being overly neurotic. Or maybe my nerves were just shattered: two minutes into the programme Number Three leaned so far over the rail that I had to pull her back by her knicker elastic. Any chance of appearing highbrow after that was going to be difficult.

Still, the children loved the idea of being able to look down on the bass drummer or get frightened out of their skins every time the cymbal crasher crashed her cymbals. I would have enjoyed it, too, if I could have relaxed long enough.

Number Three, who was sitting on my knee at one point, put her feet up on the rail and exposed her pink panties to the entire place. In the interests of modesty, I pulled her skirt down to cover her. And she pulled it up. And I pulled it down. And she pulled it up.

I could see one woman off in middle of the ocean of faces hiding her giggles behind her programme. Hot, stinging beads of sweat covered my forehead. Then came the moment when I really wanted to die. Not content with exposing herself, Number Three then started scratching herself down there. I might as well have brought along a monkey from the zoo as this child. I grabbed her hand away and distracted her attention by pointing at the happy conductor.

"I'm itchy," she said loud enough for people in Ringsend to hear.

There was period of calm for a while, as the orchestra slowed everything down. I kept a firm grip on the bag of sweets because the unwrapping of a Murray Mint just then would have killed the atmosphere. I closed my eyes to enjoy a brief moment of peace but opened them again to find Number Three doing synchronised nose-picking in time with the music. She complained bitterly when I made her stop.

Then, when I thought it was safe, I let the little imp move down the row to she-who-was-enjoying-herself-no-end while I settled in to enjoy the last five minutes. The soprano was giving it all she had. When she reached a high note, everything stopped and the place went dead quiet – except, arising out of the front row of the choir seats, the tiny voice of our Number Three who loves a singalong as much as the next gal. A ripple of laughter went around the place and even the soprano turned around to see who the budding talent was. Was I embarrassed? Did I want to fall down a hole and disappear?

By the end of it my wrist was numb from fanning, my nerves were begging for a week's retreat with a silent order of monks to recover, and our culture tanks were full to the brim for at least another year, thank you very much.

*

The cultural education of my children continues. I made them all sit down and watch "Zulu" which, amazingly, I successfully taped off the TV. Zulu is a brilliant movie. It is scary and exciting and has lots of people falling down dead and lots of brave soldiers and lots of other great boy stuff. My girls were bored stupid.

Number One played with that blooming Tamawhatsit thingy even before the first Zulu raised a feathered spear; Number Two started to play "school" in a corner of the room where we have a toy blackboard; and Number Three kept singing "Teddy Bears' picnic" which kind of killed the atmosphere for me.

There were poor Michael Caine and Stanley Baker and their men defending Rourke's Drift, in stifling heat and clammy uniforms, with hostile Zulus pouring over the hill toward them. And there was my lot, completely underwhelmed by the whole experience. Kids these days. They've no appreciation of art.

Every so often I'd stop the video and say: "Girls, girls, this bit is really good." They'd just sort of laugh at me and say, "Sure, Dad, really interesting." I hate it when they laugh at me.

They weren't laughing when I took them to the dentist for a check up, though. Nice lady though she was, the toothy doctor had some pretty hard things to say to each of them. Number One hasn't been brushing her teeth well enough, Number Two has to stop sucking her thumb because she'll end up looking like Bugs Bunny, and Number Three has a tiny spot of decay at the back of her front teeth. We were all kind of gobsmacked, especially me, because I'm the one who's supposed to supervise the brushing.

So our lives have changed in numerous ways. Now I'm brushing all their teeth twice a day. It is tiresome and it is tedious but it has to be done. I have bought a special, macho, muscle-building contraption to beef up my brushing arm. We have restricted sweet eating to Sundays only, which I know is going to kill me. And Number Two now sleeps, much like the gun-slingers of the Old West, with a glove on one hand. It's a bright red, hairy, woolly glove to stop her sucking her thumb.

To cap it all, she-who-wants-me-to-visit-Weight-Watchers went out and bought new toothbrushes that have a little battery in them to make them vibrate like crazy.

"Hey," I said, trying one out, "pretty cool and kinky."

"They're toothbrushes," she said.

"I knew that."

"And they're not for you, ninny, they're for the children."

"That's okay," I said, trying to hide the hurt. "I'm mature. I can deal with that. Don't buy anything for me, then. See if I care."

Having taken the things for a test drive, it occurred to me that they must have seemed like a really good idea on paper. So, if I may, I'd like to make two small observations known to the people who made these vibrating toothbrushes. The first thing is this. When you put toothpaste on them and then turn them on, the toothpaste wiggles right off the brush and onto the floor. I have half a tube of toothpaste in small amounts all over the bathroom floor. It's as though a flock of seagulls flew through the place on their way home from a raid on a Polo mint factory.

The second thing is this. When I eventually get the brushes onto the children's teeth, the vibrations tickle them like crazy. Has anyone at the toothbrush factory ever tried brushing someone's teeth when they're in convulsions laughing? I feel these points might be useful in designing newer versions of this toothbrush. And, no, I don't charge for this service. It's just the way I am.

Numbers Two and Three were sitting on the stairs the other morning, waiting their turn to have their teeth done. Number Three, who is four years of age, said to Number Two, who is six years old: "Paul says he's going to marry me but he's not 'cos I don't want to marry him."

Number Two said: "Well, do you like him?"

Number Three said: "Yeah, I like him, but I don't like him enough to marry him."

Number Two said: "Well, just keep him as a friend then and marry someone else."

Number Three said: "That's a good idea."

I mean, pleeeaaaasssse! Can you imagine what their conversations are going to be like in ten years time if this is what they're like now? I'm dreading the teens already, so I am. But, by God, at least they'll have white teeth.

*

I've come to the conclusion that being a stay-at-home Dad is a bit like being a country vet. The pace of life is grand. You get plenty of fresh air. There are any number of satisfying moments and no two days of the week are exactly the same. But sometimes, just sometimes, you have to do some really, really yucky jobs.

She-who's-mixed-the-Christmas-puds-already was putting the three of them to bed the other night. Number Two, whose second front tooth was very loose, brushed her teeth so hard she nearly knocked the tooth out. There was blood and hysteria everywhere. Just a normal night at bedtime in our house, really.

The child insisted that nobody was to touch the tooth and went to bed looking like Mike Tyson after Evander Holyfield had finished with him. Her parents, though, were nervous wrecks. What if the tooth came out in the middle of the night? The child would choke to death! So we devised this plan, see, that the mission, should one of us choose to accept it, would be to sneak into the bedroom just after Number Two had fallen asleep and then, using as much skill as possible, pull the tooth out. And then run like hell, naturally.

I thought this was the best plan I'd ever heard. I nodded really enthusiastically about it. But then I had to ask the question: "Eh, who's going to do the pulling?"

She-who-can-speak-volumes-with-a-single-look smiled and patted me on the shoulder: "You are."

I should have known there'd be a hitch. As I pulled on my all-black "The Lady Loves Milk Tray" clothes, I wondered why it is always me who has to do the horrible jobs.

"Because you're the man," she said, keeping watch at the door of Number Two's bedroom.

We synchronised our watches and I set off on my mission. The floor of the bedroom was a minefield of squeaky toys, any one of which could have gone off and woken the child. I got to the bed in one piece and turned on her bedside light. Out for the count and with her thumb stuck in her mouth, she didn't budge; the little white front tooth stuck out at an angle just begging to be pulled. I reached in and caught the tooth and gave it the tiniest yank. It came out first time and Number Two shot up in the bed. For a minute I thought she was going to roar the house down, but she calmed down when I took off my balaclava. I gave her a drink of water and asked her if she was okay. She nodded but was still cradling her mouth in a really funny way. I realised that she thought the tooth was still in her mouth.

"I have your tooth here," I said, holding it out for her to see.

She beamed a big smile and hopped straight out of bed and ran to the mirror.

"Cool," she said, delighted with herself, and then she ran to show she-who-gives-all-the-dirty-jobs-to-me.

At three in the morning, "Milk Tray Man" shot up in the bed, nearly dislocating his neck in the process, and remembered the tooth fairy purely by chance. I skipped in, checked that the tooth fairy had left £1 and that she'd taken the tooth away, know what I mean? Then I crawled back to bed and couldn't get to sleep for an hour and a half.

Another job which I get "because I'm the man" is cleaning the doggy doo off shoes. Number Three stepped in it and then got into the car the other day. Was I stressed, hassled and incredibly grumpy? Yes. Until, that same afternoon, I did the same thing. The guilt at having told her off was still with me the following morning. It got to me so much that I had to apologise before she went to school.

I reminded her about it and about me being grumpy. I told her that I had done exactly the same thing that afternoon, and so I was sorry for being cross, because Dads could be really silly too. End of story. We should finish brekky, get ready and go to school. The next thing she dashed from the kitchen and there was the sound of serious puking coming from the toilet. I ran in, held her hair back and apologised profusely, this time for talking about you-know-what at brekky time. In between heaving and retching, she said it was okay. This kid knows how to forgive. She gets lots of practise.

*

Never mind about house prices, I'm staring at the ugly spectre of tooth inflation. Out in the car the other day I overheard a snatch of something Number One said about prices going up every year. I thought to myself that this was a bit much, eight-year-olds discussing the property market. When I asked what they were talking about, Number Two said it was about the amount of money the tooth fairy leaves for teeth. She had a pal with her and the pal was explaining how the tooth fairy always leaves her £2.50 for each of her teeth.

My lot were visibly jealous. Our tooth fairy only leaves £1 per tooth. But they reasoned it out for themselves. Number Two's pal had only recently lost one of her teeth. Number One hasn't lost teeth in years and Number Two lost one last year. The answer was simple: Number Two's pal was obviously getting this year's rate for a tooth from the tooth fairy, whereas last year's rate was obviously a measly £1.

I said nothing, kept my head down and just kept driving. Without having to say a word, the price discrepancy between teeth in the pal's house and our house was neatly and naturally explained away. But that still left me with the tiny problem of my children expecting 150% more for their teeth from the tooth fairy in future. It looks like I'm going to have to take a certain parent out for a quiet drink and wring that certain parent's neck.

Which brings me neatly to the subject of noses or, rather, my nose. Having a large nose is an important and useful tool for raising kids. For babies it is always something to be squeezed when a Dad gets too close; to young children it gives endless fun when you put on a funny face; but as they get into the six-to-eight-year-old bracket it can be a disadvantage when it comes to smells.

I'm talking about perfume smells. They make perfume for kids, you know. These smells are made by scientists who had a bad childhood. They are designed to make parents want to fling. My lot marched in for tea the other night stinking of this cheap stuff which they'd poured over themselves down in the neighbour's house. The perfume was called Pingu after the TV penguin character. They were not impressed when I suggested it should have been called Pongu, as I ordered them into the bathroom to wash it off.

Which is not the only thing I have to get my lot to wash off themselves these days. They have now begun a snail farm. Yes, indeed, a snail farm. You need a lot of patience being a snail farmer. And there's not much in the way of excitement attached to the job, either. They set aside a space at the side of the house where they spread out large leaves on the ground. They collected all the snails they could find, or "rounded them up" as American snail ranchers might say, and kept them in their snail farm. The only problem was that we went away for a few days and when we came back all the snails had vamoosed. The children were inconsolable. My helpful suggestion that higher fences might stop them doing the same thing the next time was not appreciated.

"They can climb fences, Dad," the eldest said huffily.

"That's why you need searchlights and guard dogs."

"Very funny," she said, wiping her nose on her sleeve out of revenge.

She wasn't the only one to shed a tear this week, though. We all went to see *Anastasia*. I was in floods. You know how it's going to end with these cartoons but they always tug at the old heart strings anyway. They all loved it and want to see it again. I've promised to take them when I recover fully. Number Two said her favourite part was when Rasputin's head fell off. Charming child.

The same kid had been washed and scrubbed in the bath the other night and was about to have her hair dried. Number Two hates this part, always has and probably always will. Mother-of-all-the-Murphys was doing the drying but the child was having none of it.

"It's boring," she said.

"It's not," her mother said.

"It is."

"But it's just like being in the hairdresser's."

"In the hairdresser's you get a magazine."

*

I've been saying it for years. There is a difference between men and women in the home stakes. We had a birthday this week. Number Two was seven. For weeks I'd been wracking my brains trying to figure out what we'd get her for a present. In the end I was panicking, so I mentioned the problem to she-whose-feet-glide-over-the-earth.

"We need to think of something for Number Two, fast," I said, breathlessly.

"Relax, it's all under control."

"What do you mean 'it's under control'? The birthday is nearly on us and we've nothing bought."

"I know what she wants."

"Duh. How do you know that?"

"She mentioned it."

"She never mentioned it to me."

"Well, she didn't actually mention it; I overhead her say it."

"But I'm her stay-at-home father."

"So?"

"So I should have overheard her say it before you did!"

"Well, you didn't, so there."

I rest my case. She picked it up from the child without having to try, yet I was going around looking for ways of getting a clue without coming straight out and asking the kid. All that expensive bugging equipment in her bedroom and for what?

We bought her a Magical Moving Polly Pocket which is really an amazing toy. The only problem is that the child keeps asking me to let her have a go on it.

Don't ask me how they do it but Polly Pocket actually moves around, on her own, with just the flick of a little handle. I think they do it with magnets or something. Either way it's great. She goes to bed, walks around her house, and even goes for a boat ride. I feel sure she's going to start going out with boys soon but we'll deal with that when we come to it. If they made one for adults, say a Magical Moving Pocket Pamela Anderson, I think it would definitely sell.

Of course, having Number Two's birthday set Number Three off about her own. She's been looking forward to her fifth birthday ever since she turned four. I am regularly asked, as you know, to send out the invitations, even though we have months to go yet.

The poor child, having watched presents being opened, and seen the birthday cake, and sung the songs, came up to me dejected, wanting to know how long it was until her birthday. I told her it was about 80 days away, which was a mistake. She scratched her head and wandered off. Then she came back and said she didn't know how long 80 days was. Have you ever counted to 80, slowly, when you were trying to get out of the house to catch the shops before they closed?

Number Two still has to have her party. All we've had for her so far is a cake and some presents. The reason for the delay is that she's having a gang of her pals to the local swimming pool and then a tea party and a disco in the house. Have you any idea what I am going to look like after cavorting with dozens of seven-year-olds in a pool, serving up a birthday tea and then bouncing around the sitting room to the Spice Girls for a couple of hours? It will not be a pretty sight. I will look every day of my 39 years at the end of it. I will constitute a new sub-species of man: Homo sapiens shaggedouticus.

Already, she-who-goes-placidly-among-the-noise and I are devising ways of consoling ourselves when it's over. A takeaway and a video have been mentioned so far. I'm sure if I ham it up a bit more, some drink might get thrown in.

Speaking of consolation, Number One came in to me the other day in floods of tears. She had me worried for a minute, because I thought she'd gone over on her ankle again or fallen off her bike.

"What's the matter?" I asked.

"It's my alien in goo," she said.

"Your what?"

"My alien in goo."

"What's wrong with it?"

"The goo's gone all hard and I can't get him out," she sniffed.

Alien in goo? Is this what I can expect from the other two when they reach her age? Aliens in goo, fart cushions, chopped-off fingers and eyeballs in jelly, itching powder, and anything that involves slime, pongy smells or disgusting sucking noises? I think the problem must be me. I'm still in the Polly Pocket phase of parenting.

*

My head is still spinning. Two birthday parties in one weekend is too much. I've declared to she-who-has-will-power that I'm not going to do it again next year. No, next year they can have their birthday parties on two separate weekends.

This is what happens when you have two children born on the same day four years apart. They don't want to have their parties on the same day, as one joint affair, because that would be two easy for their parents. They want separate parties for their separate friends, because two parties are twice as much fun as one.

Number Three's party was first on Saturday last. In the morning we spent an hour or two making the chocolate Rice Crispie cakes and putting marshmallow sweets in mini cake cases with a drop of chocolate on the bottom. The cocktail sausages were collected, the balloons blown up, the Teddy Bear cake was made and iced by she-who-is-the-right-weight-for-her-height, the tables and chairs were rearranged, the banners put up, the "parcel" was wrapped in twenty layers of paper, the donkey was drawn on a big sheet of paper and the donkey's "tail" was resurrected from where I'd stuck it in the garage last year. Phew.

As it is with parties, when you have all this done, you feel like nothing more than lying down for an hour or two to recuperate. That's exactly the time the doorbell rings and the first of the children's pals start arriving. Their parents stand around and make jolly comments about how busy you're going to be and then they head off giggling to themselves, as if their turn wasn't ever going to come.

Number Three had wanted the Magic Man to come to her party ever since February when he'd been at one of her friend's parties. Every other day, I had to assure her that he really was coming. It got so bad that I started ringing him up to make sure he really was coming. Yes, he reassured me in April, he still had my booking for July. When he did come on Saturday, everything went perfectly. The guy is a pro, and a gentleman to boot. You could have taped the laughter from the group of kids and sold it as a cure-all tonic.

When the Magic Man had finished, and they'd all got their balloon swords and balloon flowers and balloon hats, we had the feast. Parents at parties are like domestic servants: they should be seen and not heard and their sole function is to keep the thing running smoothly. And so it was. I felt like Manuel in "Fawlty Towers". With a tea towel over one arm, trays of goodies in both hands, a bottle of Coke on each shoulder and bottle of Lilt balanced on my nose, to say it was busy would be understating it. Imagine a pub that was giving away free beer on Good Friday and you'll have some idea of what it was like.

After the clean up, the realisation hit us that we'd have to do it all again the next day. At least I didn't need to blow up any balloons.

Number One had decided she wanted to take all her pals to a movie and then have her party tea back at the house. We went to *Paulie*, the children's movie about the talking parrot. I thoroughly enjoyed it but, dammit, it made me cry at the end. There is no way to blow your nose and wipe your eyes with a hanky without twenty macho fathers in the rows behind you saying to themselves: "Sissy househusband!" That's why I always walk out of the cinema with my hard man waddle and a "what are you looking at, pal?" expression on my face.

The party tea for Number One was a repeat of Number Three's, except it was faster because older kids eat more quickly. After the grub we had a disco with the game of moving statutes, then musical cushions and then pin the tail on the donkey. When they'd all gone home, the two of us had to sit down for half an hour to get our breath.

I reckon that between the two parties I consumed at least half a chocolate cake, three packets of crisps, eight Rice Crispie cakes, eight chocolate marshmallows, a litre of Coke-7Up-Lilt mixed together, a quarter pound of cocktail sausages, two Toffee Crisp bars, four chewy carambars (three fruit, one caramel) and a packet of popcorn. And I don't know about you, but that kind of food always makes me hungry.

*

Now that I eat in a healthier manner, Lent holds no fear for me. I kind of like it in a weird way. Nobody looks twice at you when you say, thanks, but no cake for me, I've given it up for Lent. Or when you say, no beer for me, I'm off it for Lent. It's great. Try saying it any other time of year and it's like being transported onto the set of "Father Ted". Ah, you will, comes the response, you will, you *will*!

Curiously, I've nothing left to give up. Apart from drink, that is. And what I'm doing here is cutting it way down. Even at Communion I'm only taking the barest sip now. On the food side, I don't eat dairy products any more; that means no butters or anything made of same. No baker's yeast either, so that means no cakes, biscuits, breads or packet sauces. No salt, no malt, no ready-made meals. So you can imagine how I was stuck for something to say when the three degrees asked me what I was doing on "give up" day.

"You could stop being grumpy," Number One offered, trying to be helpful. She doesn't like it when I complain about having to Hoover the kitchen table every time she's had a meal.

"I could stop being grumpy, that's a good idea," I said. "And you could stop complaining every time you're asked to tidy your room. Or you could stop barking at me when I wake you in the morning. Or you could eat your food at mealtimes. Or you could try and keep your food on your plate at mealtimes, even."

I could have taken out my list of things she could give up but the child will only be nine for so long and I didn't want to miss any more of it than was necessary. Besides, this was only the warm-up. We still had to get down to the real business of what we'd actually give up. The reason I'm only getting around to writing this now is because I thought we'd all agreed on one thing the week before last, only to find out this week that this wasn't what was agreed at all.

In Number One's case, I thought she was giving up cakes, sweets and biscuits. As it turns out, she's only really giving up cakes and sweets. Biscuits are allowed. I found this out when I refused to take out the biscuit tin this week and was met with howls of protest worthy of a Lazio defender who's been given a yellow card.

I thought that was that until it turned out later in the week that not only is she still allowed biscuits but she's also allowing herself what are termed "sucky" sweets. "Sucky" sweets are a different breed and genus to "chewy" sweets, which have a higher enjoyment content because they are not allowed during Lent.

But that's where I was proved wrong again. Numbers Two and Three, who are going around together these days as if they were joined at the hip, both stated categorically that they were giving up – shock, horror – cakes, sweets and biscuits. But, like Number One, biscuits are now allowed; not only that, they tell me they are allowing themselves "chewy" sweets and not "sucky" sweets, of all things.

"Oh, and we're also allowed chocolate," Number Two added quickly, "because chocolate is not sweets."

God forbid, but I think these children are going to grow up to be offshore, tax-efficient, insurance bond salespersons.

The dang goldfish died. The Velvet Pom Pom will no more dance across the front of the tank like a sour-faced American cheerleader. It has Pom'd its last Pom. Like Goldie before him, there was a solemn ceremony during which the fish was slung into a hole in the flower bed and a hasty headstone erected. That bed is beginning to look like Boot Hill in the old Wild West.

The statutory twenty-second mourning period was interrupted with an offer from Siobhain the neighbour. She wanted us to have her goldfish PeeWee as a replacement because he was lonely. He just swam around and around in his bowl all day, a permanent sorrowful tear in the corner of his eye. So now we have PeeWee and he goes around and around in our square tank all day. Still, he looks happier in himself, if it's possible to be happy being a goldfish. The next stage is to negotiate visitation rights with Siobhain. I think once a week is enough, personally, but now she's saying she wants to take PeeWee out to places and be around him more, so their relationship doesn't suffer. I knew it was going to be like this.

Chapter Nine

Yes, there is a dark side to all this being at home stuff . . . And it's not very pretty, either

"Planet Earth calling Dad. Planet Earth calling Dad."

This is Number One's way of reminding me I'm not paying attention to what's going on. And could you blame me?

We'd all just got back from a visit to the doctor and I felt like I'd just run the Dublin marathon. There are some pretty obvious disadvantages when one of the children needs to be taken to the doctor. You have to put clothes without holes or stains on everybody, for one. Secondly, because I don't have a medical card, I have to pay for it. Thirdly, it means waiting in a room full of very boring magazines. Finally, it means anything from ten to twenty minutes trying to keep three children from wrecking the doctor's room.

That's where the real stress is. That's why I arrived home in a dazed state.

While he was checking out Number Three, Number One and Number Two were having a ball of a time wrestling on his high couch. I tried to ignore it but it was impossible. They were making so much noise that the people in the waiting room must have thought the bottle of laughing gas was leaking.

When I got them to stop, they sat with their hands on their knees for two whole seconds and then they jumped off the couch and started chasing each other around his desk. This went on just long enough for one of them to trip over his curtain screen. Curtain screens make a cute

noise when someone trips over them. It's like a sym-
phony orchestra falling downstairs.

I told them to stop once again, in my best Batdad,
George Clooney, I-love-you-but-you-will-die voice. So
they stopped messing for another two seconds.

Then Number Three, who was finished with the doctor, started sucking the wooden, throat examination
thingies while Number Two was being checked out. God
help anybody coming in after us who thought they were
having a sterile spatula stuck in their mouth after our
Number Three had gobbed all over them. But rest as-
sured, I have a pretty good memory of the doctor
breaking up a handful of the things as we were leaving.
At least I think I do. No, I'm sure I do.

Then it was the turn of the blood pressure pump. I
bet medical students the world over never realised the
fun uses to which such a boring old piece of equipment
can be put. My girls pumped the thing up and then let it
down again for all they were worth. It was a bit like one
of those toys that jump when you pump air into it, except it didn't jump and it was an unexciting colour. Its
owner, who by contrast was turning a much more exciting colour, didn't look so happy by then.

Just when I thought it was safe to ask a sensible
question of the doctor and await a sensible answer,
Number Three started rifling through the box of "I was
brave at the Doctor's" stickers. I was trying to focus on
the steps I should take to ensure the continuing good
health of all my children when she slapped one of these
stickers in the middle of her forehead and charged around
shouting: "Teddy Bear Power Ranger!"

I reached out, grabbed her and pulled her onto my
knee. The same could not be done with Number Two,
who was beyond my reach and jumping up and down on
the weighing scales trying to see the heaviest weight
she could register.

By this stage Number One came over to tell me she

was bored and I felt ready for a good cry. The thought crossed my mind to ask the Doc for some Valium or Prozac or tranquillisers. But, call me old-fashioned, I have a problem with giving those things to young kids.

*

Everything was going fine. It seemed like the week might rise from its usual chaotic mayhem to score an impressive "quite good, actually" on my Dad-o-meter. I was all set to sit down and write about how well the kids were doing at school, how we'd managed to stabilise the dizzying increase in the overdraft, and how she-whose-cakes-always-rise was happyish with my management of the domestic chores. Life was more than fine, it was good.

And then it happened. The phone rang. She-who-works-outside-the-home had barely been gone an hour or so. She wanted to know if I knew what day it was. I was surprised that the testing of my powers of concentration had now broadened to include spot checks. But, as this was a question I could answer, I told her what day it was. No, no, she didn't mean what day of the week it was, she meant what "day" it was. This was getting tougher, so I trotted out the day, the date, the month and the year.

Having passed this test with flying colours she then added a cunningly clever twist. Did I know what day it was yesterday. Like, duh? Of course I knew what day it was yesterday. You take one away from the date and you just count one back from the day of the week and, hey presto, you get the answer.

"Do you realise we forgot our anniversary?" she asked.

"Oh," I said.

This was a shock. Working on the basis that the best form of defence is attack, I wondered aloud how it was that having slaved, cleaned, cooked and kept house for the past year, nothing had been organised to celebrate this occasion, no dinner in a candlelit restaurant, no box of flowers or bunch of chocolates, no romantic weekend at a secluded location even? Was this any way to treat a stay-at-home spouse? Thankfully, my expert skills at blaming someone else were not needed any further. She fully accepted her part in forgetting this most momentous of occasions. Phew!

My second setback of the week was the foolish and ill-advised purchase of new weighing scales. I blame the Consumer Choice magazine for this. They recommended this battery-operated electronic gizmo as the best buy. Argos stocks it and it costs £29. I took the money out of the Post Office and off I went and bought it. When I got home I discovered I weighed half a stone more than my old-fashioned weighing scales had been telling me. No wonder the bed springs were still squeaking like mad – and this was just when I'd walk into the bedroom.

We question why people hate modern science. If scientists want to be loved a bit more they'd better stop making products like this which never, ever lie. It has ruined my entire week. Nevertheless, just as in my former working life, I will persevere. I'll just have to stay on the NuTron diet somewhat longer. That's all. It's no big deal. I can handle this.

You'd think that was enough hardship for one week, but that would be to forget the mental gymnastics which three children will put you through. Last Sunday, driving home after visiting the cousins in their new house, my question to them was simple. Who wanted beans and who wanted peas with their roast chicken?

"I want beans," said Number Two.

"I want peas," said Number One.

"I want beans," said Number Three.

"Good," I said, "that's two beans and one peas."

"No, I've changed my mind," said Number Three, "I'll have peas instead of beans."

"Okay, that's two peas and one beans," I said. "So, in that case, I'll do peas for everybody because I don't want to open a can of beans just for one. Is that alright?" I asked Number Two.

"No way," said Number Two, "I want beans, I hate peas, I won't eat them. They're disgusting."

Ignoring the overacting, I decided to drop it and just open the can of beans for the sake of peace and quiet. But it was not to be.

"That's not fair," said Number One, "you make me eat things I don't like, so she should have to eat things she doesn't like."

"No way," said Number Two, "I'm not eating peas, I hate peas, they're disgusting."

"But then that's not fair on me," said Number One.

"Can I have carrots?" Number Three piped up.

And so it went, all the way home, as our little car, chugging up hill and down dale, wound its merry way to our sweet abode, the harmonious sounds of a happy family filling the evening air with gladness, warmth and understanding. Not.

*

It was a very foolish thing for me to do. I might end up paying for it for the rest of my life. But, in my defence, she-who-is-damn-talented-and-everybody-says-so caught me in an off moment. I'd just come back from a brisk hour-long walk with the children. This consisted of pushing Number Three in her buggy up a very steep hill, playing chasing with all three of them around the top of the hill, and then playing shop with them on the way down the other side of the hill at their favourite shop-playing spot.

Did I arrive home feeling refreshed and rested and ready to think straight? No.

So, there I was, tired, sweaty and trying and figure

out how I'd cook a leg of lamb that hadn't defrosted yet, when I got called. I was being invited to inspect the work that she-who-has-the-most-fabulous-taste had been doing all afternoon, namely painting the smallest room in the house.

"What do you think?" she asked, full of expectant tension.

"I don't like it," I said far too quickly, followed by a desire to bite my tongue off.

"Why not?"

"It's that green, I think it's too dark."

There was a silence you could cut with a knife.

"Well, I mean," I continued, "maybe it won't be too dark when it's finished."

The same silence ensued.

"Maybe when the mirror is back up and the pictures are back up it'll be just fine. Yes, now that I look at it, I think it's fine. Well done. Carry on."

There is no way of backing out of situation like that. I walked away knowing that there will be many times in the years to come for me to contemplate my regret at what I had just said. Now, my only hope of redeeming myself is either to win the lottery or else become fabulously rich and famous. Failing either of these two options, I may have to try charm classes.

At least the kids still like me, most of them anyway. I think I scored major Brownie points by going out with them trick-or-treating on Hallowe'en night. I don't know if you've noticed this, but Hallowe'en teaches you a lot about people. I suspect that Hallowe'en was not invented as a night to celebrate the spirits of the dead but was, instead, invented so that we can get a good look at the kind of people who live around us.

One woman asked the children to sing her a song, so they sang "Trick or treat, smell my feet, give us something nice to eat!", which was not quite what she'd had in mind. We also called to the house of a woman I had never seen, after nearly five years in the place. She never comes out and the curtains are always pulled, so I presumed she didn't want to be disturbed. Lo and behold, she opened the door and was so happy to see kids that their bags weighed a ton when they left her.

The next house was the one we called to last year where they told us they had nothing because someone had just died. This year they had the same story, without the death in the family part. At another house the door was opened by a tall guy dressed as the Frankenstein monster, which nearly scared the children to death. Another man opened his door and swung a toy axe at them, which also nearly scared them to death. And another man asked them for their names and, when they dutifully told him, he grumbled, "Never heard of ye."

At our last house of the night, Number One gave the door knocker such a bang that it set off the house alarm, which is what you deserve if you're not at home on Hallowe'en night. That scared the children to death too. On the way home I cut a deal for a share of the goodies. When we got back they were true to their word. I got the fruit and nuts and they got the sweeties.

Goldie, our hip-hop goldfish, passed away. He now swims in that great fish tank in the sky. I scooped his stiff little body out of the water, wrapped him in tin foil and then left the girls to make the funeral arrangements. It was a quiet, private affair, just family and a few close friends. His remains lie in the flower bed with a little headstone and some flowers to mark the spot. Number Three took it very hard until I suggested we could get another fish. She looked at me, the twinkle returning to her eyes, and said: "Great, can we do it now?"

*

Life has gone through a sudden shift. Number Three has had the stabilisers removed from her bike. I found myself telling her that she was too young to have the stabilisers removed, but she kept insisting, so I took them off. Within two days she was whizzing past the house like Evel Knievel. This set me off, pining for the loss of my baby. Where had all the time gone? Pretty soon she'd meet a nice boy, fall in love, get married, big wedding, cost me a fortune. Then reality hit. I heard her crying before I saw the state of her face. I'd turned my back for a second and she'd flown down a hill on her own and came off the bike. Her nose looks like Joe Bugner's on a bad day. Okay, it doesn't mean the stabilisers are going back on, but it's a reminder to me that she's not exactly a grown-up yet.

Number One, on the other hand, is rapidly approaching those ranks. There's a song on the radio every now and again where some libidinous American lady keeps singing "I'm so horny, horny, horny..." Personally, I'm delighted for her, but it raises some thorny horny questions in our house.

"What does 'hawny' mean, Dad?" the child asked me the other day.

"'Hawny'? Oh, I think it means, I don't know, kind of, you know, kind of happy, I think."

"My friend's mum told her it means your willy gets big."

"A big willy?"

"Yeah, is that what hawny means?"

"Yeah, I suppose it is what hawny means, in a way, yes."

"But she's a girl."

"Who's a girl?"

"The girl singing the song about being hawny."

"Oh, right."

"And girls don't have willies."

"Exactly. You're right. They don't."

"So it can't mean that, can it?"

"No, it can't, can it?"

"So what does 'hawny' mean?"

"I think for girls it means excited; they get excited."

"Is that all?"

How in the name of goodness am I going to cope with complicated issues like relationships, courting, kissing, dating, contra-you-know-whatsit, birth, death, nature, existence, God and the Universe, if I can't cope with a simple question like the meaning of "hawny"? I could be wrong about this but I always assumed that I'd be a shining example of an enlightened generation of parents who would sail through all this stuff with all the right answers. Wrong. I handled it more like a parent from the late 1800s. Next time I'm going to be prepared and I'm going to face these hawny questions head on, with an answer firmly thought out and prepared: "Ask your mother."

Which is exactly what I should have done when the tape machine in my car needed fixing. Number One is a total Spice Girl but sometimes she goes at problems like a builder's labourer. One example was when she was trying to change a tape in the car radio. The thing wouldn't go in properly the first time so she forced it and forced it and forced it until I nearly drove off the road. Needless to say, I was severely stressed by the experience, so much so that it was two months before I got around to sending it in to the car radio hospital. This place is run by a chess maestro who talks in serious electronics lingo all the time. It's not a car radio, it's a H15 second generation thingy. It's not just broken, its phaser needs a transplacer with an overhead camshaft. So when I rang up to see if the patient was cured, I was really careful with the words I used.

"The name is Murphy and it's a Blaupunkt car radio that needed..."

"Oh, yeah, the blue spot."

"No, it's a Blaupunkt car radio."

"That's what I said, blue spot."

"No, Blaupunkt."

"'Blue spot' is the English for Blaupunkt."

"Oh."

If only I'd asked mother-of-all-the-Murphys. She knows a little bit of German. She could have spared me the embarrassment. But, oh no, I had to go it alone. Note to be stored away and tattooed indelibly on my brain: ask your wife first before you do anything, anything at all, no matter how small.

*

The five of us were in the car beetling down to Glendalough and the weather was gorgeous. Unusually, for our car, everything was quiet. The children had teased and giggled and shouted and sung and tickled and wrestled themselves into exhaustion. The silence was broken by a question from the older of the three aimed at she-who-must-be-pampered-at-weekends.

"How do elephants mate?"

I nearly drove off the road. I could feel the inborn male instinct to bring the car to a sudden screeching halt and run off into the woods to hug a tree.

Without blinking, my wife said: "Like the way doggies do it, love."

Let me explain. Our children are not living a cotton wool existence. They see female doggies trying to give male doggies piggybacks all the time. Not very successfully mind you, but all the fun is in the trying. So I drove on in a kind of sticky sweat knowing I'd have to say something but not sure exactly when to jump in and even less sure about what I should say. A bit like being on "The Andy O'Mahony Sunday Show".

"Does the daddy do something or do they rub bellies or something?"

"No, love," my wife went on calmly, "the daddy elephant puts semen..." (at this I gave a little jump in my seat and my left eye began to twitch) "into the mummy elephant. It's like the seeds of a plant. She has an egg inside her and when the semen and the egg come together that makes a baby elephant."

There was silence again as Number One mulled over this newly acquired knowledge. I could only imagine it. Seeds of a plant... mmm... wonder if it needs watering? Egg inside her... mmm... never seen elephant eggs. Semen... mmm... that's a new word. And then came understanding.

"You mean, like pee pee?"

"Yes, love," I spluttered, glad to be involved at last.

I gave my wife an old buddy-buddy wink. We'd been through hell and come out the other side, her and me, together. The only way to deal with these issues was to be up front and honest and...

"Is that the way human babies are made?"

I gulped again and struggled to avoid an oncoming tour bus. Had they moved Glendalough further away or what? We should have been told.

"The same way except mummies and daddies give each other a big hug," my good wife explained.

"Can the mummy get on top of the daddy instead of the daddy getting on top of the mummy?"

I was about to lighten things by saying, "Only if Daddy has been very good," but I decided to let it drop.

"Yes, love," my wife said and that, thanks be to all that's holy, was that. The child was satisfied at last, silence returned to our little car and my shirt dried out in no time once we got to the lakes.